Ordnance

Edinburgh and the Borders Walks

Pathfinder Guide

Compiled by Brian Conduit

Key to colour coding

The walks are divided into three broad categories, indicated by the following colours:

Short, easy walks

Walks of moderate length, likely to involve some uphill walking

More challenging walks, which may be longer and/or over more rugged terrain, often with some stiff climbs

Acknowledgements

I am grateful for the invaluable advice and assistance that I have received from the Scottish Borders Tourist Board, Borders Regional Council, East Lothian District Council, Scottish Natural Heritage and the Philiphaugh Estate Office, as well as the tourist information offices throughout the area.

While every care has been taken to ensure the accuracy of the route directions, the publishers cannot accept responsibility for errors or omissions, or for changes in details given. It has to be emphasised that the countryside is not static: hedges and fences can be removed, field boundaries can alter, footpaths can be rerouted and changes of ownership can result in the closure or diversion of some concessionary paths. Also paths that are easy and pleasant for walking in fine conditions may become slippery, muddy and difficult in wet weather and stepping-stones over rivers and streams may become impassable. If readers know of any changes which have taken place, or have noticed any inaccuracies, Jarrold Publishing would be grateful to hear from them.

Ordnance Survey   ISBN 0-319-00488-0
Jarrold Publishing   ISBN 0-7117-0815-0

First published 1995 by Ordnance Survey and Jarrold Publishing

Ordnance Survey   Jarrold Publishing
Romsey Road   Whitefriars
Southampton SO16 4GU   Norwich NR3 1TR

© Crown copyright 1995

Printed in Great Britain by Jarrold Printing, Norwich. 1/95

Previous page: The harbour at St Abbs, Berwickshire

Contents

Introduction to Edinburgh and the Borders

There can be few cities in Britain or indeed elsewhere that have a finer setting than Edinburgh. Its position on the southern shores of the Firth of Forth – at the eastern end of the central lowland belt between the Highlands to the north and the Southern Uplands to the south – made it the ideal site for Scotland's capital, even though it did not attain that role until the fifteenth century.

South of Edinburgh, the Border country stretches away towards the Cheviot Hills and England. Nowadays a quiet and tranquil area, it was for many centuries the bloodiest territory on the whole of the British mainland. Only its numerous castle remains, some still substantial and some meagre, and the ruins of the distinguished quartet of Border abbeys – Jedburgh, Kelso, Dryburgh and Melrose – provide visible evidence of these past conflicts.

Superb mixture of hills and lowland

This is ideal country for walking: a superb mixture of empty rolling hills and expansive moorlands, delightful river valleys and secluded lochs, bounded on the north and east by fertile lowlands and an impressive coastline. Running like a silvan thread through the heart of the region is the River Tweed, famed both for its natural beauty and its salmon fishing. Many of the Border towns are situated either near its banks or those of its many tributaries.

Apart from the coastal lowlands, the area chiefly comprises a number of lofty hill ranges that make up the eastern half of what geography textbooks traditionally call the Southern Uplands. Uplands they certainly are, with numerous summits over 2,000 feet (610 m) and the highest, Broad Law, rising to 2,754 feet (840 m). Virtually all the Border hills share the same characteristics. There are no rugged and craggy outlines and few steep ascents or severe challenges as there are in the Highlands or the mountains of the English Lake District and Snowdonia. Border hills are for the most part smooth, grassy expanses with long, undulating ridges, more akin to the Brecon Beacons in South Wales, providing extensive views and a great sense of solitude and remoteness. However, even though they may be more benign and look less forbidding than the Highlands to the north, these Border hills must still be treated with the same respect and caution, especially in bad weather.

The hills begin almost in the centre of Edinburgh itself. When strolling down Princes Street, the impressive profile of Arthur's Seat dominates the skyline, rearing above Holyrood Park at the bottom end of the Royal Mile. The short, steep climb to its 823-foot (251 m) summit provides magnificent panoramic views over the city, across the Firth of Forth, along a lengthy stretch of the Lothian coast and across the flattish terrain to the south of Edinburgh to the outlines of the nearest hills.

Nearest of all are the Pentlands, whose smooth, steep slopes extend in a roller-coaster fashion south-westwards from the southern outskirts of the city. Despite a maximum height of only 1,898 feet (579 m), the abrupt manner in which they rise above the surrounding country gives them the appearance of a mountain range. With a large number of well-way-marked paths, they provide unrivalled walking opportunities right on the doorstep of the Scottish capital.

Looking south-eastwards from the main Pentland ridge, the long lines of the Moorfoot and Lammermuir hills fill the horizon. The Lammermuirs are nearest the coast and create a broad wedge between the lowlands of East Lothian to the north and those of the Merse to the south. The Moorfoots present a steeper face and are more thickly forested, especially on their southern slopes, which descend to the Tweed valley.

South of the River Tweed lies the main bloc of the Border hills: the Tweedsmuir range, divided between the more dramatic and craggy Moffat Hills in the south and the smoother Manor Hills in the north. Here is some of the loneliest, wildest and most sparsely populated country in the Borders, where the highest summits are found. The hills surrounding the valleys of the Yarrow and Ettrick to the west of Selkirk once formed part of Ettrick Forest, a hunting ground for medieval Scottish kings; now they are a forest in the modern sense, with many of the slopes covered with conifer plantations.

To the south-east beyond Teviotdale lies the bastion of the Cheviots, straddling the border between Scotland and England. These bare and frequently windswept hills curve round to the north-east towards the coast and with the other ranges virtually enclose the western end of the Merse, the lower reaches of the Tweed, in a horseshoe of hills.

Hailes Castle above the River Tyne

Most walkers in the Scottish Borders make for the hills, but the coast and the lowlands of the Merse and East Lothian have plenty of attractions. There are many fine, bracing walks along the rugged cliffs of the Berwickshire coast; further north beyond Dunbar the coast becomes gentler, comprising a mixture of low cliffs, salt-marshes and dunes. The lowlands themselves are not flat but undulating, interspersed with low hills and punctuated with sharp, dramatic-looking volcanic outcrops: North Berwick Law, Traprain Law and the Bass Rock just off the coast, all striking landmarks that can be seen for miles around. Delightful walks can be enjoyed in the valleys of the Whiteadder Water and the River Tyne – the latter not to be confused with the Northumbrian river of the same name – and the attractive, red-tiled villages of East Lothian and the handsome and dignified buildings of Haddington are a reflection that this has always been the most fertile and prosperous agricultural region in Scotland.

Border battleground
The history of the Borders is inevitably dominated by the border itself and the long centuries of warfare and bloodshed on both sides of it. One of the main problems was that for many centuries the border was unclear and continually shifting. It was the Romans who first conceived the border by constructing Hadrian's Wall between the Tyne and the Solway, the first real frontier between south Britain, the future England, and north Britain, the future Scotland. Later they shifted their frontier northwards by building the Antonine Wall between the Forth and Clyde. After the departure of the Romans from Britain, invading Angles penetrated into south-eastern Scotland, and at its greatest extent their kingdom of Northumbria stretched from the Humber to the Forth. Edinburgh gets its name from a Northumbrian king, Edwin. Viking invaders ensured that Lothian, the northern part of that kingdom, became linked with Scotland rather than England by overrunning the area of Northumbria south of the Tweed and thus driving a wedge between the Anglian peoples.

Although the line of the border was more or less fixed by the twelfth century, repeated attempts by English kings to conquer Scotland, spirited Scottish resistance and counter-invasions, Scotland's alliance with England's traditional enemy, France, and constant raids on each other's territories by ruthless and lawless barons from both sides of the border all made this a bloody battleground for many centuries. Only with the union of the two crowns under James VI of Scotland or I of England in 1603, followed by the Act of Union between the two countries a century later, did peace finally come to the region.

Wool, farming, fishing and tourism
With peace came prosperity, and in the nineteenth century woollen industries became established in the Tweed valley, adding to the traditional occupations of farming and fishing. Later, reservoirs

were constructed in some of the valleys to serve the ever-growing needs of the industrial towns of the central lowlands, and in the present century the conifer plantations of the Forestry Commission have made a considerable mark on parts of the Borders landscape. Nowadays, tourism plays an increasingly important role in the economy of the region.

Although lacking the obvious majestic terrain of the Scottish Highlands, the Borders has much to offer the walker: extensive vistas across rolling and empty terrain, a drier climate than most parts of Scotland, fine castles and abbeys, a largely unspoilt and at times dramatic coastline, pleasant towns and attractive villages, and many fine and clearly defined ridge-top paths and moorland tracks – all within easy reach of the numerous attractions of Edinburgh. The Southern Upland Way crosses the area on its way from the Irish to the North Sea and provides a well-waymarked route across some of the loneliest stretches of the Border hills.

Sir Walter Scott, the most famous son of the Borders, loved this area, and a visit to his favourite viewpoint on Bemersyde Hill, near Melrose, will illustrate why. In front of you the distinctive, triple-peaked Eildon Hills rise above the surrounding low-lying country while below you the silvan Tweed makes a great loop around their base: arguably the finest view in the whole of southern Scotland and one that will surely whet your appetite to explore this beautiful area.

The law and tradition as they affect walking in Scotland

Walkers following the routes given in this book should not run into problems, but it is as well to know something about the law as it affects access, and also something of the traditions which can be quite different in Scotland from elsewhere in Britain. Most of it is common sense, observing the country code and having consideration for other people and their activities which, after all, may be their livelihood.

It is often said that there is no law of trespass in Scotland. In fact there is, but the trespass itself is not a criminal offence. You can be asked to leave any property, and technically 'reasonable force' may be used to obtain your compliance – though the term is not defined! You can be charged with causing damage due to the trespass, but this would be hard to establish if you were just walking on open, wild, hilly country where, whatever the law, in practice there has been a long tradition of free access for recreational walking – something both the Scottish Landowners' Federation and the Mountaineering Council of Scotland do not want to see changed.

There are certain restrictions. Walkers should obey the country code and seasonal restrictions arising from lamb-

Approaching Peebles

6

The bold profile of Salisbury Crags overlooking Edinburgh

ing or stalking priorities. Where there is any likelihood of such restrictions this is mentioned in the text, and visitors are asked to comply. When camping, use a campsite. Camp fires should not be lit; they are a danger to moorland and forest and really not necessary as lightweight and efficient stoves are now available.

In theory a persistent trespasser or someone proving a nuisance (camping or causing vandalism) can be restrained by interdict – the Scots term for the placing of a court order banning certain actions.

In reality there is no way any law can be enforced completely in the huge, empty landscape of Scotland, and legal action is almost unheard of; the system of *de facto* tolerance and mutual respect seems to have worked well. But it does depend on the visitor knowing the rules, written and unwritten, observing restraint during the stalking season, and following the country code.

Many of the walks in this book are on rights of way. In Scotland rights of way are not marked on the Ordnance Survey maps as is the case south of the border. Local planning authorities however have a duty to protect and maintain them – no easy task with limited resources. Over much of the country, nearly every major glen or lochside will be a right of way, and it was not felt necessary to show these as such on the maps – a further reflection of the greater freedom to roam that is enjoyed in Scotland. The only established rights of way are those where a court case has resulted in a legal judgment. No major attempt at closing claimed rights of way has ever been successful, though several cases have gone to the Court of Session and even the House of Lords.

So a path on a map is no indication of a right of way, and many paths and tracks of great use to walkers were built by

estates as stalking-paths or for private access. While you may traverse such paths taking due care to avoid damage to property and the natural environment, you should obey restricted access notices and if asked to leave do so. In Scotland (on rights of way) a cycle is regarded as 'an aid to pedestrianism'. A dog on a lead or under control may also be taken on a right of way. There is little chance of meeting a free-range solitary bull on any of the walks. Any herds seen are not likely to be dairy cattle, but all cows can be inquisitive and approach walkers, especially if they have a dog. Dogs running among stock may be shot on the spot; this is not draconian legislation but a desperate attempt to stop sheep and lambs being harmed, driven to panic, or lost, sometimes with fatal results. Any practical points or restrictions applicable will be made in the text. If there is no comment it can be assumed that the route carries no real restrictions.

The watchdog on rights of way in Scotland is the Scottish Rights of Way Society (SRWS), who maintain details on all established cases and will, if need be, contest attempted closures. They produce a booklet on the Scottish legal position (*Rights of Way, A Guide to the Law in Scotland*, 1991), and their green signposts are a familiar sight by many footpaths and tracks, indicating the lines of historic routes.

Scotland in fact likes to keep everything as natural as possible, so, for instance, waymarking is kept to a minimum (the Scottish Rights of Way Society signposts and Forest Walk markers are in unobtrusive colours). In Scotland people are asked to 'walk softly in the wilderness, to take nothing, except photographs, and leave nothing except footprints' – which is better than any law.

7

Key Map 1

Key Map 2

CONVENTIONAL SIGNS 1 : 25 000 or 2½ INCHES to 1 MILE

ROADS AND PATHS
Not necessarily rights of way

M1 or A6(M)	M1 or A6(M)	
A 31(T)	A 31(T)	Motorway
B 3074	B 3074	Trunk or Main road
A 35	A 35	Secondary road
		Dual carriageway
		Road generally more than 4m wide
		Road generally less than 4m wide
		Other road, drive or track

Unfenced roads and tracks are shown by pecked lines

---------------------- Path

RAILWAYS

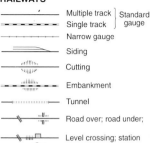

	Multiple track } Standard gauge
	Single track }
	Narrow gauge
	Siding
	Cutting
	Embankment
	Tunnel
	Road over; road under;
	Level crossing; station

PUBLIC RIGHTS OF WAY Public rights of way may not be evident on the ground

------------ } Public paths { Footpath
——— ——— }   { Bridleway

+ + + + + Byway open to all traffic
▲ ▼ ▲ ▼ ▲ Road used as a public path

The indication of a towpath in this book does not necessarily imply a public right of way
The representation of any other road, track or path is no evidence of the existence of a right of way
Public rights of way are not shown on Ordnance Survey maps of Scotland

BOUNDARIES

— · — · — · —	Region or Islands Area
— — — —	District
–◦–◦–◦–◦–	London Borough
·················	Civil Parish (England)* Community (Wales)
— — — — —	Constituency (County, Borough, Burgh or European Assembly)

Coincident boundaries are shown by the first appropriate symbol

*For Ordnance Survey purposes County Boundary is deemed to be the limit of the parish structure whether or not a parish area adjoins

SYMBOLS

♦ ♦	Place of worship {	with tower
●		with spire, minaret or dome
+		without such additions
☐ ☐		Building; important building
▨ ▲		Glasshouse; youth hostel
⬭		Bus or coach station
Ⴟ Ⴟ		Lighthouse; beacon
△ ▲		Triangulation pillar
. T; A; R		Telephone: public; AA; RAC
▨▨▨▨▨		Sloping masonry
---☐---·--- pylon pole		Electricity transmission line
◦ W, Spr		Well, Spring
⌖		Site of antiquity
⚔ 1066		Site of battle (with date)

	Gravel pit
	Other pit or quarry
	Sand pit
	Refuse or slag heap
	Loose rock
	Outcrop
	Cliff
	Boulders
	Scree

☐	Water
▨	Mud
	Sand; sand & shingle
NT	National Park or Forest Park Boundary
NT	National Trust always open
NT	National Trust limited access, observe local signs
NTS NTS	National Trust for Scotland
FC	Forestry Commission

VEGETATION Limits of vegetation are defined by positioning of the symbols but may be delineated also by pecks or dots

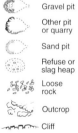

♣ ♣	Coniferous trees	◦ ◦ ◦ ◦	Orchard
△ △	Non-coniferous trees	◦– ◦– ◦–	Scrub
Ⴠ Ⴠ	Coppice		Marsh, reeds, saltings.

Bracken, rough grassland
In some areas bracken ( ) and rough grassland (······) are shown separately
Heath

} Shown collectively as rough grassland on some sheets

In some areas reeds ( ) and saltings ( ) are shown separately

HEIGHTS AND ROCK FEATURES

 50 ·
285 · } Determined by { ground survey / air survey

Surface heights are to the nearest metre above mean sea level. Heights shown close to a triangulation pillar refer to the ground level height at the pillar and not necessarily at the summit

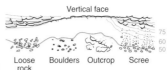

Vertical face

Loose rock   Boulders   Outcrop   Scree

75
60
50

Contours may be shown at either 5 metres or 10 metres vertical interval

TOURIST INFORMATION

 Abbey, Cathedral, Priory

 Garden

☆ Other tourist feature

 Aquarium

 Golf course or links

✕ Picnic site

X Camp site

 Historic house

 Preserved railway

 Caravan site

 Information centre

 Racecourse

 Castle

 Motor racing

 Skiing

Cave

 Museum

Viewpoint

Country park

 Nature or forest trail

 Wildlife park

 Craft centre

Nature reserve

Zoo

P Parking

𝕮𝖗𝖔𝖘𝖘
SAILING Selected places of interest

PC Public Convenience (in rural areas)

☏ T Public Telephone

𝔐 Ancient Monuments and Historic Buildings in the care of the Secretary of State for the Environment which are open to the public

⊕ Mountain rescue post

◆   ◆ National trail or Recreational Path Long Distance Route (Scotland only)

NATIONAL PARK ACCESS LAND   Boundary of National Park access land Private land for which the National Park Planning Board have negotiated public access

Pennine Way Named path

◄ Access Point

WALKS

 Start point of walk   Featured walk   ➤ Route of walk   ▪◾▶ Alternative route

ABBREVIATIONS   1 : 25 000 or 2½ INCHES to 1 MILE also 1 : 10 000/1 : 10 560 or 6 INCHES to 1 MILE

BP,BS	Boundary Post or Stone	Mon	Monument	Spr	Spring	
CH	Club House	P	Post Office	T	Telephone, public	
FV	Ferry Foot or Vehicle	Pol Sta	Police station	A,R	Telephone, AA or RAC	
FB	Foot Bridge	PC	Public Convenience	TH	Town Hall	
HO	House	PH	Public House	Twr	Tower	
MP,MS	Mile Post or stone	Sch	School	W	Well	
				Wd Pp	Wind Pump	

Abbreviations applicable only to 1 : 10 000/1 : 10 560 or 6 INCHES to 1 MILE

Ch	Church	P	Pole or Post	TCB	Telephone Call Box
F Sta	Fire Station	PW	Place of Worship	TCP	Telephone Call Post
Fn	Fountain	S	Stone	Y	Youth Hostel
GP	Guide Post				

FOLLOW THE COUNTRY CODE

Enjoy the countryside and respect its life and work

Guard against all risk of fire

Fasten all gates

Keep your dogs under close control

Keep to public paths across farmland

Leave livestock, crops and machinery alone

Use gates and stiles to cross fences, hedges and walls

Take your litter home

Help to keep all water clean

Protect wildlife, plants and trees

Take special care on country roads

Make no unnecessary noise

Reproduced by permission of the Countryside Commission for Scotland

1 Linlithgow Loch

Start:	Linlithgow
Distance:	2½ miles (4 km)
Approximate time:	1½ hours
Parking:	Linlithgow
Refreshments:	Pubs and cafés at Linlithgow
Ordnance Survey maps:	Landranger 65 (Falkirk & West Lothian), Pathfinders 405, NS 87/97 (Falkirk (South)) and 406, NT 07/17 (Queensferry & Broxburn)

General description *The highlights of this flat and easy circuit around Linlithgow Loch are the constantly changing views of Linlithgow Palace and church perched above the southern shores. From the north-east corner the views across the loch are enhanced by the distinctive shape of Cockleroy in the background.*

Two grand adjacent buildings dominate the old town of Linlithgow and all the views across the loch. The substantial ruins of Linlithgow Palace, popular residence of Stuart kings and birthplace of Mary Queen of Scots in 1542, date from the fifteenth to the seventeenth centuries. Building was started by James I of Scotland in 1425, and the work was completed around the middle of the sixteenth century. Extensions and repairs were carried out in the seventeenth century but the palace became a ruin when it was carelessly set alight by some of the Duke of Cumberland's troops in 1746, following the Jacobite Rebellion. The church next to it, one of the finest in Scotland, also dates from the fifteenth and sixteenth centuries, apart from the thin modern aluminium spire above the west tower.

The walk starts at Linlithgow Cross in the town centre. Facing the town hall, now tourist information centre, turn left along The Vennel, shortly turn right at a sign 'Public Library and Public Toilet' and then turn left down to the lochside (**A**).

Follow a tarmac path beside a picnic and play area, which later curves to the right along the west side of the loch. All the way there are superb views of the palace and church above the loch from a variety of angles. In the north-west corner, cross a footbridge and turn right at a fork to continue along the north shore of the loch. After passing the last of the houses,

the tarmac path becomes a rough path, screened from the nearby M9 by a grassy and wooded embankment on the left, but the noise of the traffic is inescapable. This is a particularly attractive stretch of the walk, at times passing between trees and gorse bushes and with superb views to the right of the palace with the prominent hill of Cockleroy beyond.

Just before emerging onto a lane, turn right (**B**) through a kissing-gate to follow a grassy path beside the east shores of the loch, bending right to continue along the south shore. The path later bears left away from the loch, beside woodland on the right, to go through a kissing-gate onto a road. Turn right and then at a sign 'Linlithgow Peel and Palace' turn right again (**C**) along a tarmac path between houses on the right and a church on the left, which heads downhill to rejoin the lochside.

Cross a footbridge and follow the tarmac path to the left to continue along the south side of the loch towards the palace and church. At a path junction below the palace ruins, turn left along an

Linlithgow – church and ruined palace above the loch

uphill path, later turning right to pass between the palace and church. Turn left through the palace gateway known as The Fore, built for James V around 1535 to give access to The Peel or outer enclosure of the palace, to return to the start. □

2 Moorfoot and Hirendean Castle

Start:	South side of Gladhouse Reservoir, on lane by reservoir notice ½ mile (0.75 km) north-west of Moorfoot
Distance:	2½ miles (4 km)
Approximate time:	1½ hours
Parking:	Wide verge by notice for Gladhouse Reservoir
Refreshments:	None
Ordnance Survey maps:	Landranger 73 (Peebles & Galashiels), Pathfinder 434, NT 25/35 (Leadburn & North Middleton)

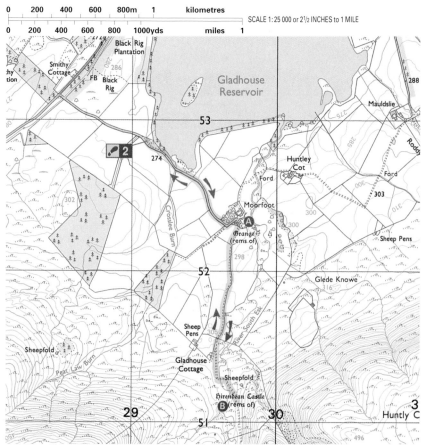

The scanty remains of Hirendean Castle stand in a lonely setting in the Moorfoot Hills

3 Dunbar and John Muir Country Park

Start:	Dunbar
Distance:	3½ miles (5.5 km)
Approximate time:	2 hours
Parking:	Dunbar
Refreshments:	Pubs and cafés at Dunbar
Ordnance Survey maps:	Landranger 67 (Duns, Dunbar & Eyemouth), Pathfinder 409, NT 67/77 (Dunbar)

General description *It is appropriate that the impressive stretch of coastline to the east of Dunbar, an area of cliffs, dunes and saltmarsh, should have been created a country park named after John Muir for this native of Dunbar was one of the pioneers of the national parks movement in the USA. This short and relaxing walk explores part of the country park, following a well-waymarked trail along the cliffs from Dunbar Harbour to Belhaven Bay and returning to the town by way of a quiet road.*

Refer to map overleaf.

General description There is a remote feel about this short and easy walk in the Moorfoot Hills. From the southern shores of Gladhouse Reservoir you walk along a lane into the hamlet of Moorfoot and then follow a track beside the infant River South Esk to the fragmentary remains of Hirendean Castle, dramatically situated at the foot of the hills where the valley narrows. On the return there are grand views over the reservoir to the line of the Pentlands.

With the reservoir to the left, walk along the lane into the hamlet of Moorfoot and, a few yards after the tarmac lane ends, turn sharp right (**A**) along a track at a 'Private Road' notice. Follow the track over two cattle-grids and continue through the valley of the South Esk, enjoying the superb views of the Moorfoots and narrowing valley ahead with the ruins of Hirendean Castle seen on the east slopes of the valley. At a fork just before a cottage, take the left-hand, lower track, which soon turns left to cross the river. Head up to the castle ruins which, though sparse, occupy a fine, atmospheric position at the foot of the hills from where there are dramatic views of the Moorfoots, the South Esk valley and across the reservoir to the Pentlands (**B**).

From here retrace your steps to the village of Moorfoot and turn left along the lane to return to the start. □

With fine sandy beaches and an attractive location, Dunbar has become a popular seaside resort but it is also a historic town. Of the great castle – one of the most important medieval fortresses in Scotland – only a few crumbling walls survive above the harbour, but the High Street contains the imposing seventeenth-century Town House and the birthplace of John Muir, now a museum. He was born in 1838, emigrated to America with his family at the age of eleven and later played a major role in the creation of the Yosemite and other national parks.

Begin by the harbour and make your way to the fragmentary ruins of the castle at its west end. Just before reaching them, turn sharply left, almost doubling back, and then turn equally sharply right to walk along an uphill paved path. The path turns first left and then right to pass in front of Dunbar Leisure Pool at the start of a waymarked Clifftop Trail.

Continue along this paved path, which bears left to a road, turn right, turn right again (**A**) and after a few yards turn left along Bayswell Park. Where the road ends, bear right along a paved path, passing to the left of a war memorial. Now continue along a paved esplanade that

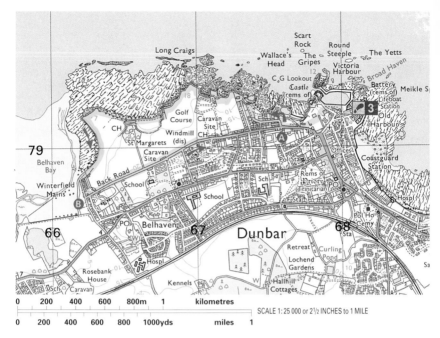

| 0 | 200 | 400 | 600 | 800m | 1 | kilometres |
| 0 | 200 | 400 | 600 | 800 | 1000yds | miles | 1 |

SCALE 1 : 25 000 or 2½ INCHES to 1 MILE

twists and turns above the rocky coast, giving fine views to the right of Dunbar Castle and ahead to Bass Rock, Traprain Law, North Berwick Law and the wide, sandy expanse of Belhaven Bay. This Clifftop Trail is marked by a series of information boards. Turn left down steps, then down some more and turn right to continue along a path by the right-hand edge of a golf-course and above a stony beach.

The path follows the curve of Belhaven Bay sharply to the left, continuing above the bay and still alongside the edge of the golf-course, later bearing right to reach the end of a lane by a group of wooden chalets. Follow the lane as it bends left to Shore Road car park and shortly afterwards take the first turning on the left (**B**).

The road heads steadily uphill, then levels off. Follow it for 1 mile (1.5 km) back to Dunbar. ☐

Dunbar Castle and harbour

4 Dirleton and the Lothian coast

Start:	Dirleton
Distance:	6 miles (9.5 km)
Approximate time:	3 hours
Parking:	Dirleton
Refreshments:	Pub and tearooms at Dirleton
Ordnance Survey maps:	Landranger 66 (Edinburgh & Midlothian), Pathfinder 396, NT 48/58/68 (North Berwick)

General description *This flat walk starts in an outstandingly attractive village with a medieval castle and continues by way of tracks and field paths to reach the coast at*

Yellow Craig. It then follows a delightful ramble across dunes and along the edge of sandy beaches with fine views across the Firth of Forth to the Fife coast. For much of the way two well-known land-marks dominate the skyline: Bass Rock and North Berwick Law.

Dirleton must rank as one of the most attractive villages in Scotland, with eigh-teenth- and nineteenth-century cottages grouped around a spacious green that lies between the medieval castle and seven-teenth-century church. The castle is not only a fine and well-preserved building itself but is enhanced by its surroundings of yew trees, seventeenth-century bowling-green and colourful and well-tended flower borders. It became a ruin after its capture by General Monk in 1650, during Cromwell's invasion of Scotland.

Begin by heading across to the church, pass to the right of it and walk along the straight, partially hedge-lined track.

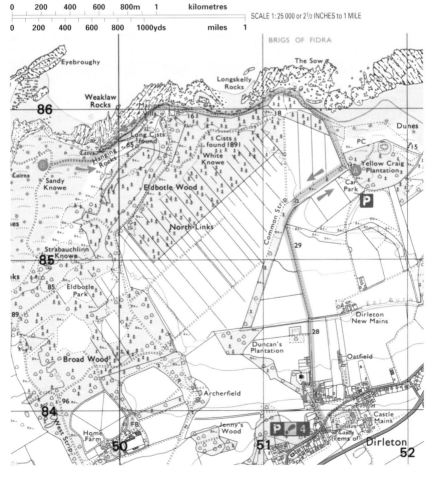

SCALE 1:25 000 or 2½ INCHES to 1 MILE

Where the track bends right, keep ahead along a grassy track between fields. To the right are fine views of both North Berwick Law and Bass Rock. On the far side, bear right to continue along the left-hand edge of a field, by a wire fence bordering woodland on the left, and turn left to climb a stile in that fence.

Continue through a narrow belt of trees to go through a gate and turn right along the right-hand edge of a field, now by a wire fence bordering woodland on the right. In the field corner go through a fence gap, turn right along a sandy path to a crossing of paths, keep ahead for a few yards and then turn left (**A**) along a track to the coast.

On reaching the sea, turn left and, keeping to the right of scrub and trees all the while, follow a sandy path across the dunes or, where the path disappears at times, walk along the edge of the beach. This is a most attractive stretch of coast with fine views across rocks and sand of the Firth of Forth and with the hills of Fife on the horizon. You can turn back at any time, but for the full walk continue to where the coast bears left and pass to the right of a large house, before descending to walk along the beach below cliffs. A concrete post marks where a path bears left uphill over the dunes and across the neck of the headland to where there is a fine view at the top over Gullane Bay (**B**).

From here retrace your steps back to Dirleton. On this return leg there are particularly good views of both Bass Rock and North Berwick Law and, on approaching Dirleton, a superb view across the fields to the castle with the line of the Lammermuir Hills beyond. □

The imposing remains of Dirleton Castle

5 Roslin Glen

Start:	Roslin Glen Country Park
Distance:	4 miles (6.5 km)
Approximate time:	2½ hours
Parking:	Roslin Glen Country Park
Refreshments:	Pub at Roslin
Ordnance Survey maps:	Landranger 66 (Edinburgh & Midlothian), Pathfinder 420, NT 26/36 (Penicuik & Dalkeith)

General description *Below the village of Roslin the River North Esk flows through a dramatic, narrow, steep-sided and thickly wooded glen, part of which is now a country park. The first half of the walk follows an undulating path through the glen, and the return leg is along a track and lane above it, from which there are fine views of the long profile of the Pentland Hills. Near the end you pass the unusually ornate Roslin Chapel, well worth a visit.*

Start by taking the path that runs parallel to the river, turning left to reach the riverbank at a footbridge. Cross the bridge over the North Esk, continue along an uphill path through woodland and, at the bottom of a flight of steps, turn right (**A**) to pass under the bridge that leads to the sparse remains of the medieval Rosslin Castle, largely destroyed by the English armies of Henry VIII in 1544, partially restored in the early seventeenth century and destroyed again by the English, this time under Cromwell, in 1650.

Descend via steps to a stone stile and footpath sign to Polton and turn left over the stile to start the walk through the thickly wooded glen. This is a superb walk through beautiful woodland, carpeted with bluebells in spring, and at times the cliffs on both sides of the glen are virtually perpendicular. After passing through a gap in a fence, you initially climb above the glen to reach a crossing of paths near the top edge of the woodland. Turn right here along a path that descends steeply, zigzagging in places, to the bottom of the glen and turn left to continue by the river. Later the path heads quite steeply uphill to a stile. Climb it and continue along the top of the glen. There is a fine view through the trees on the right of the mainly seventeenth-century Hawthornden Castle on the other side of the gorge.

After a while the path descends again to continue just above the river, with more open views to the left across fields.

Soon after climbing a stile, you emerge from the wooded glen and follow the river round a right-hand bend to another stile. Climb that and turn left away from the river to follow an uphill path between trees and gorse bushes to a crossing of paths (**B**). Turn left, head uphill through gorse onto a narrow ridge, between Roslin Glen to the left and Bilston Glen to the right, and continue steeply uphill along this narrow and crumbly ridge. At a fork, take the left-hand path and climb a stile onto a track on the edge of woodland.

Turn left along the track that keeps along the left edge of woodland, curving left. Later come fine views to the right of the Pentland Hills. Go through a metal gate and continue along a tarmac farm track – later a lane – into Roslin. Bear left to cross a bridge over a disused railway and continue through the village to a crossroads (**C**).

Turn left, and ahead is Roslin Chapel, which overlooks the glen. It was built in the fifteenth century by the Earl of Orkney as a large collegiate church but only the choir was ever completed. The chapel is unusually flamboyant for a later medieval Scottish church, resembling contemporary churches in southern Spain or Portugal – and is particularly noted for its elaborate and intricate carvings.

The River North Esk flows through Roslin Glen

Just before reaching the chapel, the route turns right, in the direction of the 'Castle', downhill along a tarmac track. At a footpath sign for Polton, turn left along a walled track that bears right downhill back into the wooded glen. In front of a metal gate by the castle, head down a flight of steps to rejoin the outward route and retrace your steps to the start. ☐

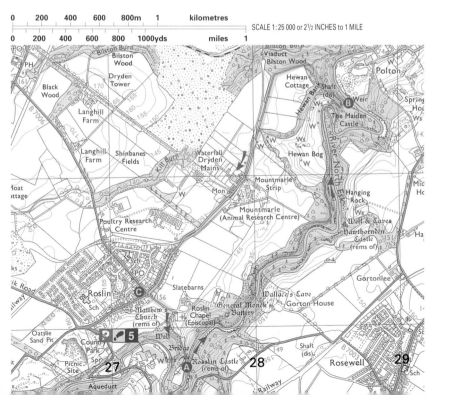

0   200   400   600   800m   1   kilometres
0   200   400   600   800   1000yds   miles   1

SCALE 1:25 000 or 2½ INCHES to 1 MILE

6 Peniel Heugh

Start:	Harestanes Visitor Centre, 1 mile (1.5 km) east of Ancrum
Distance:	3½ miles (5.5 km)
Approximate time:	2 hours
Parking:	Harestanes Visitor Centre
Refreshments:	Tearoom at the visitor centre (open April–October)
Ordnance Survey maps:	Landranger 74 (Kelso), Pathfinder 474, NT 62/72 (Jedburgh)

General description *This well-waymarked route starts at the Harestanes Visitor Centre, converted from a former sawmill and open from the beginning of April to the end of October. It climbs steadily through woodland to reach the summit of Peniel Heugh at 774 feet (237 m), a magnificent viewpoint crowned by the Waterloo Monument. On both the ascent and descent, gaps in the trees reveal grand views across the Border country to the Cheviots, and there is much fine woodland near the start and finish of the walk.*

Turn right out of the car park along a tarmac drive, shortly continuing along an enclosed path parallel to the drive. Follow this path as it turns right (**A**) to continue through woodland – a most attractive route with some fine ancient trees lining the path.

At a finger-post, turn right to cross a footbridge over a burn and turn left at another finger-post (**B**) to continue along a tree-lined path to reach the tarmac drive to Monteviot House, seat of the marquesses of Lothian, to the right. Turn left along the drive to a road, cross over and continue along the drive opposite. At a fork in front of a house, continue along the right-hand track and, about 50 yards

The Waterloo Monument on the summit of Peniel Heugh

(46 m) further on, turn right onto a track that winds along the right edge of woodland, ascending steadily and bearing left into the trees to reach a lane (**C**).

Turn right and almost immediately turn left to continue quite steeply uphill through trees. Gaps in the trees on the right reveal superb views over the Teviot valley to the Cheviots beyond. At a fork, continue along the left-hand track and at the next fork continue again along the left-hand track. On nearing the edge of the woodland, the Waterloo Monument can be seen straight ahead.

A few yards before emerging from the trees, bear left along a track that continues uphill through woodland, curving right to reach a kissing-gate. Go through, turn left, continue uphill by a wall on the left and, where the wall bends left, keep straight ahead to reach the monument (**D**). This is a magnificent all-round viewpoint, with the winding Teviot below and the Eildons and Cheviots standing out prominently. The 150-foot- (46 m) high monument was erected by the sixth Marquis of Lothian to commemorate the Duke of Wellington's victory at the Battle of Waterloo and was started soon after the battle was fought in 1815. Around it are the remains of some of the earthworks of two forts: one Iron Age and one from the Dark Ages.

Retrace your steps to descend through the woods as far as the first finger-post (**B**). Here do not follow the outward route to the right but keep ahead, in the direction of the 'Visitor Centre', along another attractive tree-lined track. Look out for where waymarks direct you to the right off the track to continue along a path by a burn on the right. Cross a footbridge over the burn, continue to a tarmac track and turn right along it to return to the start. ☐

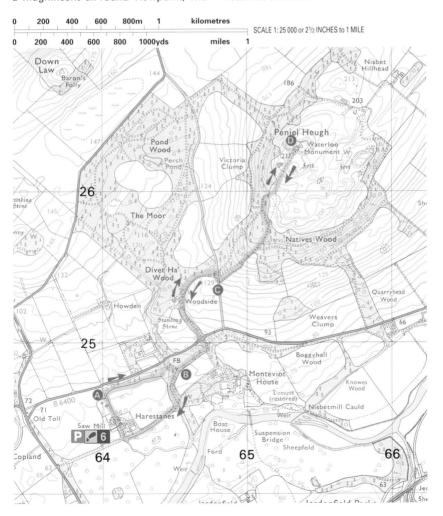

SCALE 1:25 000 or 2½ INCHES to 1 MILE

7 St Mary's Loch

Start:	Southern end of St Mary's Loch
Distance:	7½ miles (12 km)
Approximate time:	3½ hours
Parking:	Parking areas at the southern end of the loch and several laybys along the A708
Refreshments:	Pub and café at the southern end of the loch
Ordnance Survey maps:	Landranger 73 (Peebles & Galashiels), Pathfinder 472, NT 22/32 (Yarrow & St Mary's Loch)

General description *St Mary's Loch, 3 miles (4.75 km) in length, is the largest and, many would argue, the most attractive loch in the Border country. This walk does a circuit of it, using the Southern Upland Way along its eastern shore and mostly following the road along its western shore. On the circuit, the views*

St Mary's Loch

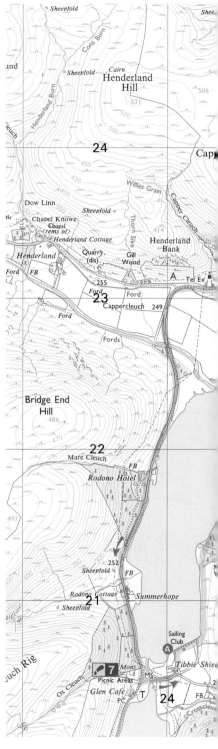

Sheepfold

Old Kirkstead

FB

Dry Cleuch

Hut Circles &
Enclosure

Dryhope Tower
(rems of)

Sheepfold

Kirkstead
Hill

Sheep Pens

Sheep
Pens

Dryhope

439

Kirkstead

Herton's
Hill

FB

519

Law

Grouse Burn

Dryhope Haugh

C 250

B Sheepfold

250

Cairn

E

D

250

Sheepfold

Sheep Shelter

Southern Upland Way

Thorny Rig

Brockie Sike

St Mary's Loch

Bowerhope

Captindish Terraces

387

FBs

Sheepfold

Whitson Sike

Sheepfold

Sheep Pens

Peat Law

Bowerhope
Law

478

Coom Sike

Bowerhope Burn

Coom Shank

521

Cairn

Hass Sike

Sheepfold

561

Sheepfold

589

March Sike

392

Sauchie Law

504

Nether Hill

427

Sheepfold

392

Craggy Sike

Cairn

The Wiss

589

Cairn

osscleuch

Southern Upland W

Ford

25

26

Thirlestane Head

27

Sheepfold

Thirlestane Brae

0   200   400   600   800m   1   kilometres

0   200   400   600   800   1000yds   miles   1

SCALE 1:25 000 or 2½ INCHES to 1 MILE

across its sparkling and tranquil waters to the encircling steep-sided hills are constantly changing, and the route is both easy to follow and undemanding. The only climb is a short, steep one to the superb viewpoint of St Mary's Kirkyard above the western side of the loch.

Start at the southern end of the loch near the monument to James Hogg (1770–1835), known as the Ettrick Shepherd, and the most famous of the Border poets and a close companion of Sir Walter Scott. Take the road between St Mary's Loch and the adjoining Loch of the Lowes to Tibbie Shiels Inn, a well-known and historic hostelry frequented, among others, by Scott and Hogg. Cross a bridge, turn left at a Southern Upland Way sign to walk through the inn car park and go through a kissing-gate at the far end (**A**). Now follow a well-waymarked path along the east side of the loch, over a series of stiles, enjoying the superb views across the water all the while. After passing a farm on the right, join and continue along a farm track below conifers.

Nearing the end of the loch, Dryhope Tower, a peel or fortified tower, can be seen peeping above the trees on the opposite side. Demolished on the orders of James VI at the end of the sixteenth century, it was later rebuilt but fell into ruin again. Soon after passing the end of the loch, the track curves left (**B**) to cross a bridge over the River Yarrow and keeps ahead to the road. Turn left and, about 100 yards (91 m) after crossing a bridge over a burn, turn right through a gate (**C**), a few yards beyond the wall corner, and turn left along a pleasant, grassy path, parallel to the road and lochside on the left. From this path come more fine views over the loch, and as an alternative you can sometimes walk beside the loch when the water-level is not too high.

Pass through several gates and, when you see a stile and public footpath sign to St Mary's Churchyard below, turn right at a crossing of paths (**D**) for a brief but worthwhile diversion, following a grassy path steeply uphill and bearing left to reach the churchyard (**E**). This place offers possibly the finest view over the loch. The church was destroyed by fire in 1557 and never rebuilt but the churchyard still remains.

Retrace your steps downhill, climb the stile onto the road and turn right along it. Follow the road for just over 2½ miles (4 km) to return to the start. After a left bend past Clappercleuch, there are good verges and more fine views through the trees across the loch. ☐

8 Arthur's Seat and Duddingston Loch

Start:	Palace of Holyroodhouse, Edinburgh
Distance:	3½ miles (5.5 km)
Approximate time:	2 hours
Parking:	Car park just beyond entrance to palace
Refreshments:	None on the way but plenty in Edinburgh
Ordnance Survey maps:	Landranger 66 (Edinburgh & Midlothian), Pathfinder 407, NT 27/37 (Edinburgh)

General description *There is a ruggedness and sense of remoteness on parts of*

this walk in Holyrood Park that makes it difficult to believe that you are within the city boundaries of Edinburgh, scarcely a stone's throw from the bustle of Princes Street. Despite its modest height of 823 feet (251 m), the climb up to Arthur's Seat is quite steep and exhausting but the view from the top surpasses that of many higher peaks, stretching right across Lowland Scotland and along the Lothian coast. After descending, the route continues by way of the village of Duddingston and beside Duddingston Loch. The final section over Salisbury Crags gives particularly dramatic views of the irregular jumble of buildings and spires that create the picturesque skyline of Scotland's capital.

Refer to map overleaf.

The Palace of Holyroodhouse at the bottom end of Edinburgh's Royal Mile began life as the guest house of Holyrood Abbey, substantial portions of which survive on its north side. It was begun by James IV in 1501, but most of the present building dates from the late seventeenth century when it was rebuilt by Charles II following destruction. Holyrood Park was originally the park attached to the palace. With the steep, rocky, volcanic slopes of Arthur's Seat and the three lochs around its base, it gives the impression that a piece of the Highlands has been transported to the suburbs of Edinburgh.

Begin by crossing the road from the car park into the park and turning left along a gently ascending tarmac track. St Margaret's Loch is soon seen ahead. The track curves right. At a fork, take the left-hand path that descends slightly into the flat, grassy valley known as Dry Dam or Long Row. On the hill ahead are the scanty ruins of St Antony's Chapel, overlooking the loch.

Bear right (**A**) along a clear, grassy path for the ascent of Arthur's Seat. At first the

View along the Lothian coast from Arthur's Seat

path climbs steadily through the valley, making directly for the blunt, prominent bulk of Arthur's Seat; later the going becomes steeper. Follow the path as it veers left, climbs a series of steps and continues more gently upwards across the face of the hill, before bending sharply to the right for the final leg to the summit, marked by a triangulation pillar and view indicator (**B**). The all-round views are magnificent, taking in the Lothian coast with Bass Rock, the Lammermuir and Pentland hills, Firth of Forth, Fife coast and the Old Town of Edinburgh, the latter dominated inevitably by the castle.

Start the descent by retracing your steps to where the path bends sharply to the left. Here leave the outward route by keeping ahead in the direction of Dunsapie Loch below, descending easily along a broad, smooth, grassy path to reach the road that encircles the park, opposite a car park and just to the right of the loch. Cross the road and, in the right-hand corner of the car park, turn right along a path that skirts the base of the hill on the left. At a fork, take the right-hand path downhill towards a wall, turn right

alongside the wall and descend a long a flight of steps to a road (**C**). If you wish to visit Duddingston village – a rural enclave with a twelfth-century church perched above the loch – turn left. Otherwise, turn right along the winding road above Duddingston Loch on the left and later below the almost perpendicular, rocky, gorse-covered slopes of Samson's Ribs on the right.

Bear right off the road (**D**) along a grassy path to follow the base of the slopes as they bear right, heading gently uphill towards the prominent jagged outlines of Salisbury Crags, to reach the park circular road again. Turn right for a few yards and, where the road bends right, turn sharp left (**E**) onto a stony track that heads steadily uphill, flattens out and then descends quite steeply across the face of Salisbury Crags. This is the Radical Road, constructed in the 1820s allegedly to provide work for the unemployed, and from it there are superb views to the left across Edinburgh.

The track continues to reach the circular road opposite the car park and the starting point.

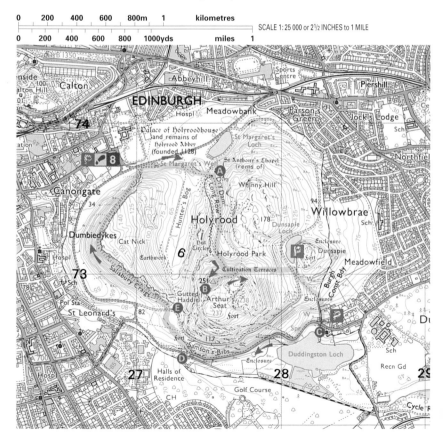

9 Monks Road and Cap Law

Start: Nine Mile Burn

Distance: 4½ miles (7.25 km)

Approximate time: 2½ hours

Parking: Nine Mile Burn

Refreshments: None

Ordnance Survey maps: Landranger 65 (Falkirk & West Lothian), Pathfinders 419, NT 06/16 (Livingston & Currie) and 433, NT 05/15 (West Linton)

General description This fine, fresh, open walk on the eastern slopes of the Pentland Hills ascends Cap Law by way of the Monks Road, an ancient and well-defined path, to reach the base of the main Pentland ridge below West Kip. On the almost parallel descent, there are superb views ahead across the lowlands of the North Esk and South Esk rivers to the distant line of the Moorfoots and Lammermuirs. Route-finding could be difficult in bad weather and misty conditions.

In the corner of the car park at Nine Mile Burn, go through a gate at a public foot-path sign for Balerno via Braid Law and take the enclosed track ahead. This is part of a Roman road. At a right-of-way sign in front of a gate, turn left and head uphill along the right-hand edge of a field, by a

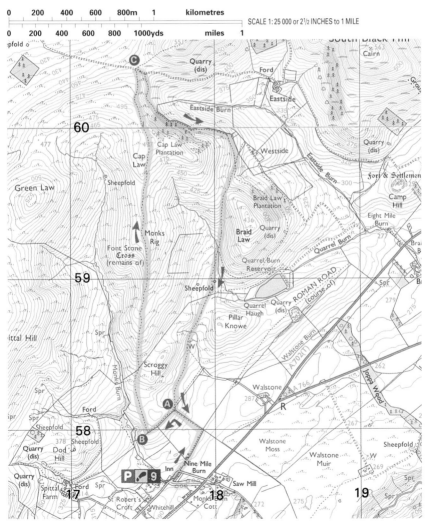

0   200   400   600   800m   1   kilometres
SCALE 1:25 000 or 2½ INCHES to 1 MILE

0   200   400   600   800   1000yds   miles   1

wall on the right, to climb a stone stile in the top corner (**A**).

Turn left alongside the wall on the left and, a few yards after passing a stile on the left, turn right (**B**) at the end of a clump of gorse onto a faint but discernible path that heads gently uphill across grass, parallel to a narrow valley on the left and making for the rounded peak ahead. Climb a stile in a wire fence just in front of a wall, go through a gap in the wall and continue steadily uphill along the clear path ahead, the Monks Road, over Scroggy Hill, Monks Rig and Cap Law. There are grand views ahead across smooth, grassy slopes of the main ridge of the Pentlands. The path heads towards the base of the prominent peak of West Kip and eventually descends to a stile. Climb it and turn right along a track just below West Kip.

After about 100 yards (91m), turn right (**C**) over the next stile, at a public footpath sign for Nine Mile Burn, along a path that bears left and contours the side of the hill, passing below a small plantation. Follow the path gently downhill, bear right on joining another path, by another public footpath sign for Nine Mile Burn, head over the shoulder of a hill and then

Looking across to the Moorfoot Hills from the southern slopes of the Pentlands

continue gently downhill below the slopes of Braid Law on the left. Ahead there are magnificent views across the lowlands to the line of the Moorfoot Hills, and on the right is the ridge traversed on the outward route.

Climb first a stile in a wire fence, then a stone stile in the wall immediately ahead and bear right to continue along a clear path across grassland and bracken, eventually heading slightly uphill to a wire fence and beyond it to a wall and stone stile (**A**). Climb the stile, here rejoining the outward route, and retrace your steps to the start.   ☐

10 Coldingham Bay and St Abb's Head

Start:	Coldingham Bay, ¾ mile (1.25 km) east of Coldingham village
Distance:	6½ miles (10.5 km)
Approximate time:	3½ hours
Parking:	Coldingham Bay
Refreshments:	Beach café (seasonal) at Coldingham Bay, pub at St Abbs, café at Northfield Farm
Ordnance Survey maps:	Landranger 67 (Duns, Dunbar & Eyemouth) Pathfinder 423, NT 86/96 (Eyemouth & Grantshouse)

General description There are some spectacular coastal views on this walk, which starts from the sandy curve of Coldingham Bay and continues by way of the fishing village of St Abbs around the sandstone cliffs of St Abb's Head, a nature reserve. As a contrast, the inland return route takes you beside a tree-fringed loch, passes the nature reserve centre and goes through the village of Coldingham with its priory remains, but nowhere are you more than ½ mile (0.75 km) from or out of sight of this glorious rugged coastline.

Refer to map overleaf.

Start by walking down a tarmac track to the fine beach at Coldingham Bay and turn left along the edge of it. At the far end of the beach, climb steps to the cliff top and turn right to follow a tarmac path for the short distance to St Abbs.

In the village, bear right along a road between single-storey houses and turn right at a T-junction (**A**) along a road that curves left above the harbour to another T-junction. Turn left, passing to the right of the prominent church, and at a footpath sign to St Abb's Head turn right (**B**) along a path, between a wire fence on the left and a wall on the right. After passing through a metal kissing-gate, the path turns left and later curves right to continue as a cliff-top route with superb views of the spectacular rocky coastline. The winding path is clear and easy to follow, initially keeping to the cliff top, later descending into a grassy valley below the cliffs and ascending again to regain the cliff top.

Continue to the lighthouse on St Abb's Head, bear left (**C**) to pass to the left of the lighthouse cottage and descend to a tarmac road. Before you continue along the road, a brief detour along a narrow path up the small hill to the left provides a magnificent view along the Berwickshire and Lothian coasts and inland to the Cheviots and across the Border country.

Walk along the winding, narrow road, descending above Mire Loch and bending to the left.

Before reaching a cattle-grid, turn left (**D**) across grass towards the loch, climb a stile to the left of a gate and continue along a pleasant winding path through reeds, gorse, rough grass and stunted trees. The path climbs steadily, and from

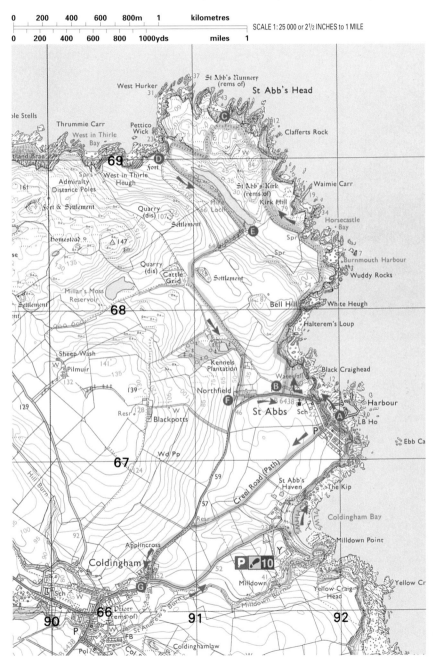

SCALE 1:25 000 or 2½ INCHES to 1 MILE

The sandy curve of Coldingham Bay

it there are fine views to the left over Mire Loch and ahead to the sea. The loch is man-made, created by the building of a dam in 1900. On joining a track at the far end of the loch, turn right (**E**) uphill to rejoin the lighthouse road at a bend and keep ahead along it, following it around several bends to Northfield Farm (**F**), a nature reserve centre. St Abb's Head is a National Nature Reserve, owned by the National Trust for Scotland and managed in co-operation with the Scottish Wildlife Trust. It is of national importance for its plant life and geology and especially as a nesting-place for large numbers of sea-birds.

Turn left through the car park, walk past the picnic area and farm buildings to climb a stile onto a road and follow the road back through St Abbs, temporarily rejoining the outward route. After passing above the harbour, the outward route turns left along Murrayfield, but here keep straight ahead (**A**) along Creel Road. The road soon ends, but continue along a most attractive, grassy, undulating path, enclosed and later tree-lined, to reach a road.

Turn left along the road into the village of Coldingham, whose church incorporates parts of a medieval priory, originally founded in the eleventh century and repeatedly attacked and damaged during the many wars between Scotland and England.

On the edge of the village, turn left (**G**) along a road signposted to Sands and follow it back to the start. For most of the way there is a parallel footpath to the left of the road. ☐

11 Ettrick valley

Start:	Ettrick
Distance:	4½ miles (7.25 km)
Approximate time:	2½ hours
Parking:	On verges west of Ettrick, near James Hogg monument
Refreshments:	None
Ordnance Survey maps:	Landranger 79 (Hawick & Eskdale), Pathfinder 484, NT 21/31 (Ettrick)

General description *Despite its short length, this is quite a demanding walk with some steep climbing and rough walking across open, pathless moorland. From the Ettrick valley the route follows the Southern Upland Way, climbing beside Scabcleuch Burn to reach the head of that valley. The return descent uses a waymarked right-of-way but the path is not visible on the ground, and the going is rough and boggy in places. This walk is not recommended in misty conditions, but in fine weather the views, especially* those from the higher parts of the walk, are superb.

The walk begins by the monument to James Hogg, the 'Ettrick Shepherd', well-known local poet, author and friend of Sir Walter Scott, who was born near here in 1770 and is buried in Ettrick churchyard. Facing the monument, turn left along the lane for 1 mile (1.5 km) through the Ettrick valley, passing the war memorial and early nineteenth-century church. Where the lane curves left just after crossing a burn, turn right (**A**) at a public footpath sign to St Mary's Loch and a Southern Upland Way finger-post. Climb a stile and head steeply uphill across grass to climb another stile in the top right-hand corner of the field.

Continue less steeply across open moorland, above Scabcleuch Burn on the right, climb a stile and ascend steadily and easily to the head of this narrow and steep-sided valley, enjoying the grand, sweeping views over a bare and open landscape. At the top, the path curves right to a stile. Climb it and keep ahead to reach a Scottish Rights of Way metal footpath sign (**B**). In front is a fine view of the head of the valley of Whithope Burn.

Descending towards Ettrick church

34

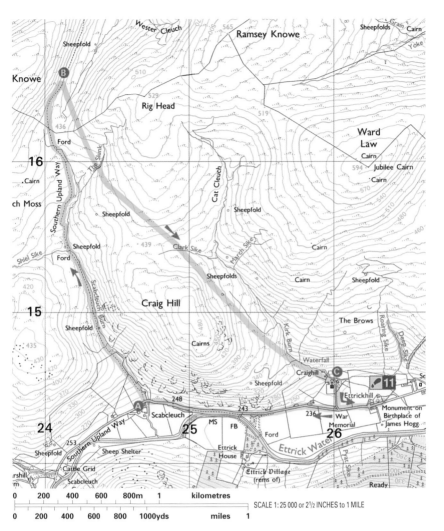

At the sign, turn sharp right in the direction of Ettrick Kirk, almost doubling back, along a faint path across rough and boggy, grassy moorland, heading for a stile in the fence ahead about 100 yards (91 m) to the left of the previous one crossed on the Southern Upland Way. Climb it – there is another Scottish Rights of Way metal footpath sign here – and continue along a rather indistinct path, almost parallel at this stage with the outward route but on the opposite side of Scabcleuch Burn, to ford a small burn. On this part of the walk the ground is likely to be rather soggy.

From now on there is no visible path as the route heads across open, pathless, rough grassy moorland. Continue in the same direction as before – south-easterly – over Craig Hill on the right, bearing gradually right. Keep to the right of the upper valley of Kirk Burn, seen below the towering slopes of Ward Law on the left, and make for the gap between Craig Hill and Ward Law. Several small burns have to be forded, and the badly drained, rough moorland is likely to be wet and boggy.

Now you descend above the valley of Kirk Burn, with a grand view over the Ettrick valley ahead, and later Ettrick church is seen below. Head down towards the church, picking up a definite grassy path through the bracken on the lower slopes, which descends steeply to a gate to the left of the church (**C**). Go through, continue downhill towards a farm, go through a metal gate and walk along a track, which bends right, passing between a house on the left and the church on the right. Continue to the war memorial and then turn left along the lane back to the starting point. □

12 Whiteadder valley and Edin's Hall Broch

Start: Abbey St Bathans

Distance: 5 miles (8 km)

Approximate time: 2½ hours

Parking: Riverside car park nearly ½ mile (0.75 km) south-east of church at Abbey St Bathans

Refreshments: Restaurant by car park

Ordnance Survey maps: Landranger 67 (Duns, Dunbar & Eyemouth), Pathfinder 422, NT 66/76 (Abbey St Bathans)

General description An Iron Age broch spectacularly situated above the valley of Whiteadder Water is the main focal point of this relatively short and undemanding walk in the foothills of the Lammermuir Hills. The route is through or above the well-wooded valley with attractive riverside stretches, splendid views across the valley to the Lammermuirs and only a few modest climbs.

The origins of Abbey St Bathans are uncertain but there is alleged to have been a Christian settlement here since the seventh century, and the mainly eighteenth-century church, about ½ mile (0.75 km) from the starting point, incorporates part of a medieval priory.

Start by walking up to the road and turn left along it, heading steadily uphill. At a right-hand bend, turn left (**A**) through a gate, at a public footpath sign, onto a path that descends steeply to cross first a footbridge over Eller Burn and then a stile. Turn left beside the burn, but the path

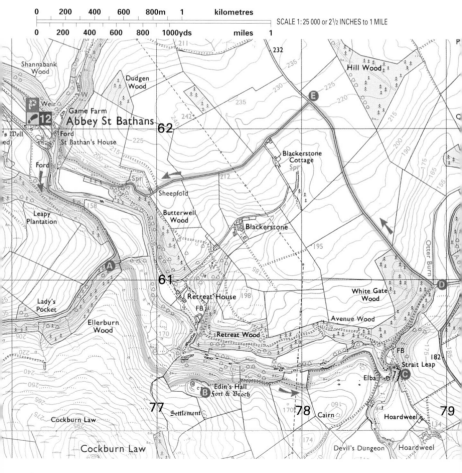

The impressive remains of Edin's Hall Broch

soon bears right and heads uphill across open grassland above the valley of Whiteadder Water to a gate. Go through, follow the direction of a waymark to the left and head downhill, by a wire fence on the left, towards the river. Go through another gate and turn right to continue by a wire fence on the right.

Look out for a yellow waymark on a fence post, which directs you to the left. Continue above a line of scrub and gorse on the left to reach the remains of Edin's Hall Broch (**B**), impressive both in their size and extent as well as for their superb position on the slopes of Cockburn Law, high above the wooded Whiteadder valley and looking towards the Lammermuir Hills. This was a large, circular, stone defensive structure, one of the few such Iron Age brochs in southern Scotland, surrounded by a complex system of earthworks.

From the broch continue along a path that heads downhill across a field to a metal kissing-gate in a wall. Go through, continue by a wire fence bordering woodland on the left, climb a stile and keep ahead along a grassy ridge to another stile. Climb this, turn left downhill by a wall on the left and turn right in the field

corner to continue above the river, by a wire fence on the left. Follow the curve of the river to the right to enter trees and reach a gate. Go through, follow the path to the left to pass to the left of a cottage and bear left again to cross a rather shaky suspension footbridge over Whiteadder Water (**C**). From the bridge there are dramatic views as the river flows through a virtual gorge at this point.

Walk along the track ahead, which bends right and continues through attractive woodland to a road (**D**). Turn left along it for 1 mile (1.5 km), heading steadily uphill, and at a sign 'Blakerston, The Retreat' turn left (**E**) along a tarmac drive. Where the drive turns left, keep ahead along a broad, walled track, which later winds downhill towards the river and becomes pleasantly tree-lined.

Before reaching the river, look out for a waymarked stile on the right, climb it and bear left along a path that soon curves right and heads uphill between gorse bushes to a gate. Go through, and the path winds through trees high above the river before descending to a track and footbridge. Turn left to cross the footbridge over the river and turn left again to return to the start. ☐

13 Kelso, Roxburgh and the River Teviot

Start:	Kelso
Distance:	8 miles (12.75 km). Shorter version 3½ miles (5.5 km)
Approximate time:	4 hours (1½ hours for shorter version)
Parking:	Kelso
Refreshments:	Pubs and cafés at Kelso
Ordnance Survey maps:	Landranger 74 (Kelso), Pathfinder 462, NT 63/73 (Kelso)

General description *The River Teviot is one of the main tributaries of the River Tweed, and this walk follows a particularly attractive stretch of it from near the confluence of the two rivers at Kelso, past the fragmentary remains of the once powerful Roxburgh Castle, to the disused railway viaduct by Roxburgh village. Although this 'there and back' route is quite long, the going is easy along clear and well-waymarked paths.*

With a spacious cobbled square lined by dignified buildings and dominated by a Classical town hall, with its fine position on the north bank of the River Tweed crossed here by an elegant bridge built by Rennie in 1803, and the remains of a medieval abbey, Kelso is one of the most attractive and interesting Border towns. Kelso Abbey was founded by David I in 1128 but fell victim to repeated English invasions and was finally destroyed in 1545. Only the west tower and western transepts remain standing to their full height but they clearly reveal the magnificence of what was the largest of the Border abbeys.

Start in The Square, face the town hall and turn right along Bridge Street, passing the abbey ruins. Cross Kelso Bridge, and to the right is a view of the vast eighteenth- to nineteenth-century Floors Castle, seat of the dukes of Roxburghe. Turn right (**A**) beside the Tweed, along the road signposted to St Boswells and Selkirk, and after passing the confluence of the two rivers continue beside the Teviot.

Follow the road to the right to cross the bridge over the Teviot and, just after passing a cottage on the left, turn left over

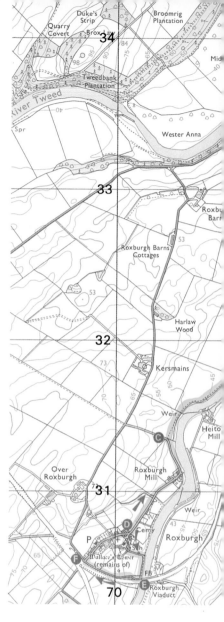

a stone stile (**B**) and turn right along a path that shortly descends steps to the river. Continue along a riverside path and, after bending left, you pass below the scanty remains of Roxburgh Castle, once a powerful royal residence occupying a ridge between the Teviot and Tweed and guarding the important Royal Burgh of Roxburgh. In such a strategic Border area, Roxburgh was continually attacked by English armies and frequently changed hands between Scotland and England. James II of Scotland was killed by the bursting of a cannon while trying to recapture the castle from the English in 1460, and shortly afterwards his widow

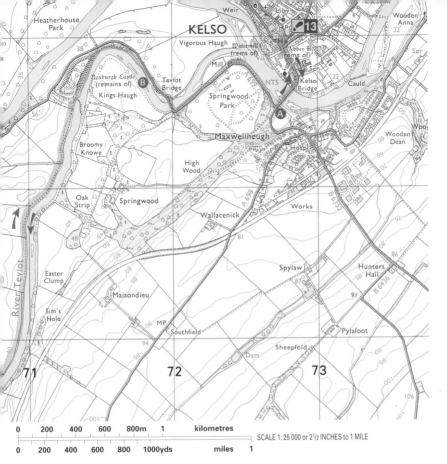

ordered it to be dismantled. The town was later destroyed by Edward VI in 1550 and it has now entirely vanished; the present village of the same name is on a different site. From the castle mound there is a particularly impressive view of Floors Castle.

Those doing the shorter version should return by retracing their steps from here.

Continue along the riverside path, a most attractive route, tree-lined in places and with fine open views across the surrounding countryside. Look out for where you turn right through a gate – immediately after climbing a stile – then turn left to continue along the left-hand edge of a field above the river, eventually following the field edge round to the right and turning left over a stile onto a lane (**C**).

Turn left along the lane into Roxburgh and, on the edge of the village, turn left along a track (**D**). The track turns left towards the river and then bends to the right to follow the Teviot up to the impressive but disused railway viaduct. In front of the viaduct, turn right (**E**) along a track that heads gently uphill, between the wooded railway embankment on the left

and a hedge on the right, to a road. The ruins seen in the field on the right are of Wallace's Tower, allegedly the remnant of a thirteenth-century tower built by the Scottish patriot William Wallace.

Turn right (**F**) through the village, passing the sturdy-looking eighteenth-century church, to rejoin the outward route and retrace your steps to Kelso. ☐

The site of Roxburgh Castle above the Teviot

14 Peebles and the River Tweed

Start:	Peebles
Distance:	7½ miles (12 km). Shorter version 4 miles (6.5 km)
Approximate time:	3½ hours (2 hours for shorter version)
Parking:	Peebles
Refreshments:	Pubs and cafés at Peebles
Ordnance Survey maps:	Landranger 73 (Peebles & Galashiels), Pathfinders 448, NT 24/34 (Peebles) and 460, NT 23/33 (Innerleithen)

General description *Much fine riverside walking is to be found on this well-waymarked route, which explores some of the most attractive stretches of the Tweed valley to the west of Peebles,* mostly using riverside and field paths, woodland tracks and part of a disused railway line. The first half of the walk follows the north bank of the river upstream, passing below Neidpath Castle, to Manor Bridge and on to Lyne Bridge. The return is along the south side of the valley, and there are fine views all the way. The shorter version only goes as far as Manor Bridge.

'Peebles for pleasure' states the old saying, and the town is certainly an excellent touring and walking centre, situated on the banks of the River Tweed and surrounded by wooded hills and open moorlands. It has a good range of shops, eating-places, hotels and guest-houses as well as attractive riverside gardens and a promenade. Peebles is an ancient town, once an important ecclesiastical centre, although there is not much evidence of this apart from the tower of a twelfth-century collegiate church and the remains of a friary, Cross Kirk, founded by Alexander III in 1261. These lie in a peaceful and secluded setting on the north side of the town. The friary became the parish church until being abandoned in 1783,

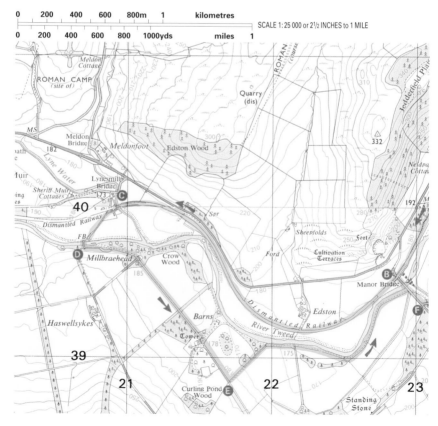

SCALE 1:25 000 or 2½ INCHES to 1 MILE

and its Victorian successor is situated at the top end of High Street, its tower and crown spire dominating most of the views of the town.

Start by this church and turn down towards the river. Do not cross Tweed Bridge but turn right down a tarmac drive, passing to the right of a swimming-pool and on to join a riverside path. Cross a footbridge over a tributary stream and continue by the Tweed through Haylodge Park, passing a metal footbridge (Victoria Bridge).

At the end of the park, continue along the riverside path to Neidpath Viaduct. This is a delightful stretch of the walk: the Tweed flows between steep, thickly wooded banks, the path dips up and down and passes below the ruins of Neidpath Castle in a dramatic situation above the river. The castle is essentially a fourteenth-century tower-house, modernised in the seventeenth century. It was besieged and captured by Cromwell's armies in 1650.

At the disused viaduct (**A**), climb a stile to the right of it, go up steps and bear right at the top, in the 'Tweed Walk, Lyne Station' direction, to continue along the

Neidpath Castle and the River Tweed

bed of the former railway track. The track eventually descends to go through a gate onto a road just to the right of Manor Bridge (**B**).

The shorter version turns left over the bridge and rejoins the full walk on the other side.

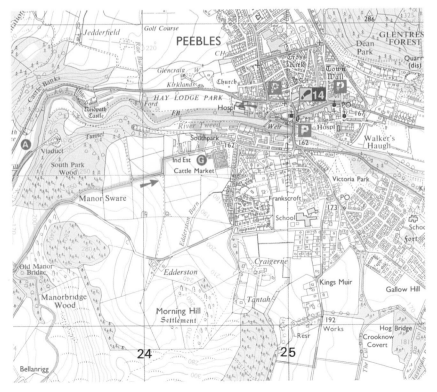

Cross the road, climb the stile opposite, climb steps to rejoin the disused railway track and continue along it, climbing several stiles. After crossing a bridge over Lyne Water, turn left down steps to a lane (**C**) and turn right along it. The tarmac lane soon becomes a rough track, and at a fork take the right-hand path that leads to a footbridge over the Tweed. Turn left over the bridge and turn left again (**D**) along a path that keeps along the edge of riverside woodland and continues through trees to a track. Bear right along the gently ascending track and, after passing the end of a road, keep ahead along a straight, tree-lined track. The track later keeps along the left inside edge of woodland and emerges from the trees to pass Barns Tower, a fifteenth-century peel tower – beyond is its eighteenth-century successor, the more comfortable and elegant Barns House.

Continue along the track as far as a Tweed Walk footpath sign, which directs you to turn left (**E**) over a stile and walk along the left-hand edge of a field, by a wall on the left. Head down to climb a stile, continue along a track to climb another one and turn right to keep along the south bank of the river. Now comes another delightful stretch of riverside walking across tree-fringed meadows, climbing several stiles, to reach Manor Bridge again.

Turn right up steps beside the bridge, climb a stile onto the road and turn right along it. Take the first turning on the left (**F**), cross Old Manor Brig, dated 1702, and continue along an uphill lane. Behind there are lovely views of the Tweed valley. At a Tweed Walk sign near the top, turn left beside a gate and, at a fork a few yards ahead, take the right-hand path, between a wall on the right and a wire fence bordering woodland on the left to reach a stile. At this point there is a superb view of Peebles ahead, lying in the valley backed by the surrounding wooded hills. Climb the stile, head downhill along the right-hand edge of a field, by a wall and later a wire fence on the right, climb another stile and continue along an enclosed track, following it around left- and right-hand bends to join a tarmac road.

Walk along the road and, after passing two side-roads on the left that both lead into a small industrial estate, turn left (**G**) through a kissing-gate into a field and walk across it to a waymarked stile at the far, narrow end. Climb the stile, take the path ahead, go through a gate and continue down to reach the river opposite Victoria Bridge. Turn right along the tarmac riverside path to return to the start. □

15 Hailes Castle and Traprain Law

Start:	East Linton
Distance:	6½ miles (10.5 km). Shorter version 3½ miles (5.5 km)
Approximate time:	3½ hours (2 hours for shorter version)
Parking:	Around The Square at East Linton
Refreshments:	Pubs and cafés at East Linton
Ordnance Survey maps:	Landranger 67 (Duns, Dunbar & Eyemouth), Pathfinder 408, NT 47/57 (Haddington)

General description *A pleasant footpath along the banks of the River Tyne leads from East Linton to the attractively sited ruins of Hailes Castle. From here the shorter version returns directly to East*

Linton along a quiet lane, but the full walk takes in Traprain Law (725 feet)(221 m), the distinctive, conical-shaped hill that rises abruptly above the lowlands of East Lothian and which can be seen for miles around. Apart from the short but steep climb to the summit of Traprain Law, this is an easy and fairly flat walk.

Refer to map overleaf.

The walk starts in The Square by the church. Walk down Bridge Street to a T-junction, turn right under a railway bridge and a few yards ahead turn sharp left at a notice 'Private Road, Pedestrian Right of Way only', along a tarmac track that heads down to the river. Turn right at the bottom onto the riverside path.

Pass under the A1 to continue along this most attractive, narrow path beside the River Tyne. Part of the route is through woodland. At one stage you climb steps above the river – from where there is a lovely view of the Tyne below and Traprain Law in the background – later descending steps to rejoin the riverbank, to continue along the edge of sloping meadows. Climb a stile to walk through some more trees, passing below a sheer cliff-face to reach a footbridge by Hailes Mill (**A**). Turn left over it and follow the uphill path ahead to a lane. Keep ahead along the lane to the mainly thirteenth-century remains of Hailes Castle, formerly the seat of the earls of Bothwell, which occupy a fine position above the river. Mary Queen of Scots stayed here in 1567 as the new wife of the Earl of Bothwell; he was her third husband and one of the conspirators involved in the murder of her second husband, Darnley.

The shorter walk returns along this quiet, narrow lane to East Linton, rejoining the full walk at **G**.

Just before reaching the castle, turn left (**B**) along a track in front of a house, pass beside a metal gate and continue between trees. After emerging from the woodland, the track ascends and bends to the right to continue between a wall on the left and wire fence on the right. Follow it around several bends, at a fork turn left along a hedge-lined track and pass beside a metal gate onto a road (**C**). Turn left towards Traprain Law, heading gently uphill.

Climb a stile on the right, bear left and

The valley of the River Tyne dominated by the conical bulk of Traprain Law

43

follow the fairly clear path that zigzags steeply uphill – there are several footpath markers – to the summit of Traprain Law (**D**). The steep climb is well worth the effort because the magnificent view from the triangulation pillar and summit cairn encompasses a long stretch of the Lothian coast from Dunbar to the Firth of Forth, the fertile Lothian lowlands and the line of the Lammermuir and Pentland hills. The summit is crowned by an Iron Age hill-fort, the headquarters of the Votadini tribe who inhabited most of south-eastern Scotland. The Votadini apparently collaborated with the Roman conquerors, and the fort seems to have been used continuously up to the fifth century AD, when it was abandoned around the time that the Angles moved into the area. In 1919 a remarkable hoard of Roman silver was found here.

Descend from the summit but at the bottom – before reaching the stile used earlier – turn right along a path that keeps parallel to the wall and road on the left. Climb a stile in the wall corner and descend steps onto the road by a parking-area. Turn right along the road for nearly 1 mile (1.5 km), at a T-junction (**E**) turn left gently uphill and at a right-hand bend turn left (**F**) along a narrow lane, signposted Kippielaw. Follow it around several sharp bends as it descends to a T-junction (**G**) and turn right along a narrow lane above the winding River Tyne as far as another T-junction.

Turn left, cross the A1, continue along the road opposite down into East Linton, passing under a railway bridge to a T-junction.

Turn left to cross a bridge over the river, follow the road to the left and, before reaching a railway bridge, turn right up Bridge Street to return to The Square. □

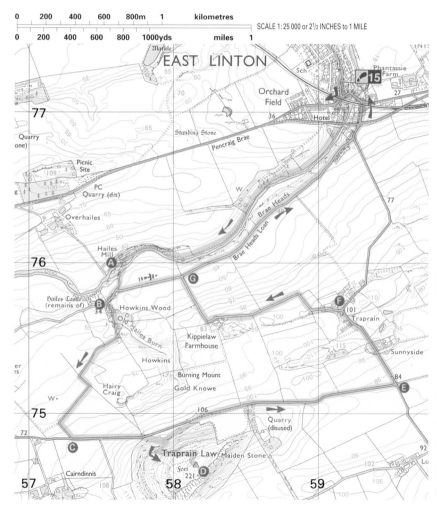

16 Glentress Forest

Start:	Glentress Forest. Off A72, 2 miles (3.25 km) east of Peebles
Distance:	5½ miles (8.75 km)
Approximate time:	3 hours
Parking:	Falla Brae car park in Glentress Forest
Refreshments:	None
Ordnance Survey maps:	Landranger 73 (Peebles & Galashiels), Pathfinders 448, NT 24/34 (Peebles) and 460, NT 23/33 (Innerleithen)

General description *This is an energetic walk, with some steep ascents and descents, through the conifer plantations of Glentress Forest on the southern slopes of the Moorfoot Hills overlooking the Tweed valley. There are fine vistas of the thickly wooded forest itself, and gaps in the trees reveal some superb views over the Tweed valley and the barer slopes of the Moorfoots further north.*

Refer to map overleaf.

With your back to the toilet block, take the blue-waymarked path through the conifers and, at a T-junction of paths, turn sharp right (**A**) to head steeply uphill. To the left there are grand views through the trees over the Tweed valley. On reaching a track, turn left and, after about 50 yards (46 m), bear right, still following blue waymarks, along an uphill path over Cardie Hill (**B**). The felled area at the top provides fine open views over both the forest and Tweed valley.

The path curves right to a track. Bear right along it to a junction of several tracks and bear right again. Shortly turn left along a steadily ascending track and for most of the rest of the route you follow black-waymarked posts. Bear right on joining a track and, a few yards ahead and just in front of a red-waymarked post, turn left along an uphill path. The path later heads downhill to pass through a gap in a wall onto a track. Ahead is a superb view over the smooth, open slopes of the Moorfoots.

Turn right along the track and, at a fork a few yards ahead, take the right-hand track that heads steadily uphill again. At a 'Dunslair Heights Viewpoint' sign (**C**), continue gently uphill to eventually emerge into open country and keep ahead to the masts on Dunslair Heights (**D**) – another magnificent viewpoint.

Retrace your steps to the Dunslair Heights sign (**C**) and turn left, following black waymarks again, along the path. Go through a gap in a wall and turn right along a path by a wall on the right, first heading gently over Caresman Hill and then continuing downhill, at first gently and later more steeply.

Look out for where a waymarked post directs you to the right along a narrow but clear path that winds steeply downhill to a track. Turn sharp right and after a few yards sharp left to continue along a steep-

Looking across the Moorfoots from Glentress Forest

ly descending path to a T-junction. Turn right, continue down to a track, turn left along the right-hand and lower of the two tracks in front but just before the track bears left, look out for a waymark which directs you to the left along a path. The path continues downhill, later runs parallel to the track on the right and eventually joins it.

Turn left by a parking and picnic area and shortly bear right along a path that bends to the right to cross a footbridge over a burn and continues across a causeway between two ponds. Do not cross a second footbridge but turn left (**E**) along a path beside the lower of the two ponds. Cross another footbridge and follow the path back to the start. □

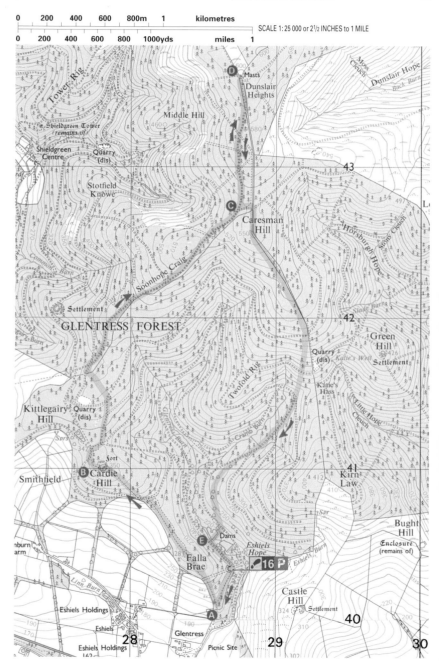

17 Haddington and the River Tyne

Start:	Haddington
Distance:	8½ miles (13.5 km)
Approximate time:	4 hours
Parking:	Haddington
Refreshments:	Pubs and cafés at Haddington
Ordnance Survey maps:	Landranger 66 (Edinburgh & Midlothian), Pathfinder 408, NT 47/57 (Haddington)

General description *After a steady climb along a road onto the lower slopes of the Garleton Hills, the route continues along a track and lane, with fine views across the Tyne valley to the Lammermuirs, later descending to join a disused railway track. The next stage of the walk follows the track for just over 2½ miles (4 km) to the edge of Haddington and, after a short section through a modern housing area, the final stretch is a delightful walk beside the placid, tree-lined River Tyne.*

Refer to map overleaf.

Many handsome and dignified eighteenth- and early nineteenth-century houses reflect the former prosperity of Haddington, which lies in the centre of some of the most fertile agricultural land in Scotland. The most impressive building is the fourteenth- and fifteenth-century collegiate Church of St Mary, cathedral-like both in its design and proportions, with a fine west front and spacious interior. It has a most attractive setting, overlooking a bend in the River Tyne and the picturesque sixteenth-century Nungate Bridge.

Start at the eighteenth-century Town House and walk along Market Street to a crossroads and traffic lights. Turn left along Hardgate and, where the main road turns right, keep ahead to the A1. Cross over and take the road ahead, signposted to East Garleton and Drem, climbing steadily onto the gorse-covered slopes of the Garleton Hills.

Just before reaching the top, turn left (**A**) along a path that soon becomes attractively hedge- and tree-lined, with fine views to the left over the Tyne valley to the Lammermuir Hills. On the hill to the right is the Hopetoun Monument. The path later broadens out into a track to reach a road. Cross over, continue along the lane ahead and, where it bears left

St Mary's Church beside the Tyne at Haddington

downhill, take the narrow lane to the right (**B**) and follow that downhill. Turn right at a T-junction, continue around several sharp bends, turn left (**C**) at a 'Railway Walk' sign and turn left again into Cottyburn car park.

Turn left (**D**) onto the track of the disused Long Niddry to Haddington branch of the North British Railway Company, opened in 1846, closed in 1968 and later converted into a cycle and walking track. Follow this pleasant, peaceful, tree-lined track for just over 2½ miles (4 km) to the edge of Haddington, passing under four bridges – including the A1 – and eventually reaching a road by a new housing estate. Cross the road, keep ahead along the track and just before the next bridge, bear left off it and head up to a road (**E**). Turn right, cross the bridge and continue down to the main road.

Cross over and take the tarmac track opposite to join a road after 50 yards (46 m). Continue along it through a new

SCALE 1: 25 000 or 2½ INCHES to 1 MILE

housing area down to a T-junction, turn left and almost immediately turn right along Long Cram. Follow the road as it curves left and, just after passing a road to the right, look out for a path between garden fences and turn right onto it. The path turns left and continues along the right-hand edge of an open grassy area, by a wire fence on the right, to reach the River Tyne (**F**).

Bear left to walk beside a tranquil, mostly tree-lined stretch of the river. After turning right to cross a footbridge by a weir, continue along a tarmac path and cross a road to the left of Waterloo Bridge. Now comes a particularly memorable final section as the river curves to the left around a wide meadow, passing St Mary's Church, to reach Nungate Bridge.

Continue along the road past the bridge, bearing left to a crossroads, keep ahead, passing to the left of the George Hotel, and walk along High Street to the start. □

18 Arnton Fell

Ordnance Survey maps: Landranger 79 (Hawick & Eskdale), Pathfinder 508, NY 49/59 (Hermitage & Saughtree)

Start:	Second layby on the right – it has a seat – along the lane to Steele Road, ¾ mile (1.25 km) from the B6399
Distance:	5½ miles (8.75 km)
Approximate time:	3 hours
Parking:	At layby
Refreshments:	None

General description *Both on the long, gradual ascent of Arnton Fell and the return route along its lower slopes, there are superb views of Liddesdale with the formidable walls of Hermitage Castle standing out prominently. This is a most enjoyable and exhilarating walk, partly on rough moorland paths and partly on easy tracks, in one of the loneliest and most*

SCALE 1: 25 000 or 2½ INCHES to 1 MILE

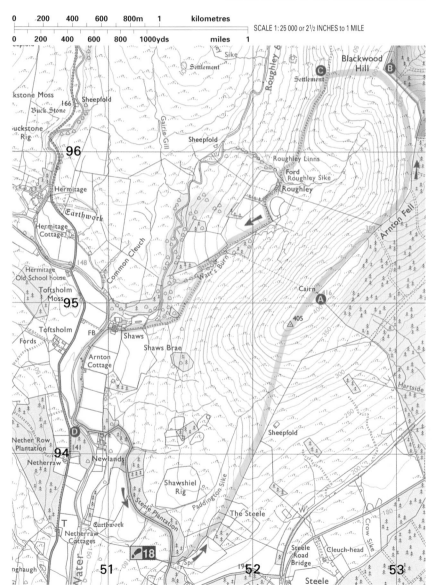

remote parts of the Borders – indeed amidst such bleak and empty expanses it is best not to attempt it in poor visibility.

Almost opposite the layby there is a stile beside a gate with a Roman helmet waymark. Climb it, immediately bear left off the track ahead and walk across grass to keep alongside a wire fence on the right. Where the fence turns right, continue along the left edge of Steele Plantation to a stile, climb it – here rejoining the fence – and head steadily uphill beside it onto the open grassy slopes of Arnton Fell.

Go through a gate, continue along the uphill path, bearing left away from the fence and climbing more steeply to reach a triangulation pillar. From here walk along the superb, broad, grassy summit ridge to a cairn by a fence corner (**A**). The magnificent all-round views from this point take in Liddesdale, Newcastleton, Hermitage Castle, the Cheviots and the Border Forest. Continue on an undulating route beside a wire fence on the right for just over 1 mile (1.5 km), keeping beside a plantation on the right to where the fence bordering the plantation bends sharply to the right (**B**).

At this point, turn left and, with Hermitage Castle directly ahead, descend steeply across rough grass to reach a track (**C**). Turn left and follow it for 2 miles (3.25 km) to a lane. It is a winding track that goes through several gates and passes two farms – there is a small, man-made loch by the first farm – gradually descending all the while. Finally, keep by a stream and later Hermitage Water and, on reaching the lane, turn left (**D**) for nearly 1 mile (1.5 km) gently uphill to return to the start. □

Liddesdale from the slopes of Arnton Fell

19 Dryburgh Abbey, Wallace's statue and Scott's View

Start:	Newtown St Boswells
Distance:	8½ miles (13.5 km)
Approximate time:	4 hours
Parking:	Newtown St Boswells
Refreshments:	Pubs at Newtown St Boswells
Ordnance Survey maps:	Landrangers 73 (Peebles & Galashiels) and 74 (Kelso), Pathfinders 461, NT 43/53 (Galashiels & Melrose) and 462, NT 63/73 (Kelso)

General description Apart from an unavoidable ¾ mile (1.25 km) stretch along a main road, this Tweed valley walk is on woodland and riverside paths, quiet lanes and minor roads. There are four main focal points on the route: Dryburgh Abbey (involving a brief but worthwhile detour), Wallace's statue, Scott's View and the Tweed bridges at Leaderfoot. Dryburgh has probably the most beautiful setting of all the Border abbeys, Scott's View is generally acclaimed as the finest in Scotland south of the Highlands, the walk starts and finishes in a wooded glen and there is an attractive stretch beside the River Tweed. All this adds up to a fine and varied walk with plenty of scenic attractions and much historic interest. There is quite a lot of 'up and down' work but mainly steady and gradual.

Refer to map overleaf.

The walk starts in front of the Railway Hotel opposite the Royal Bank of Scotland building. Turn down Tweedside Road, turn left at a footpath sign 'To the Glen' along a tarmac track that turns right and heads downhill. Go under the bypass and at a waymarked post ahead continue along the path into Bowden Glen.

Cross a footbridge over a burn to a path junction (**A**) and continue ahead through the attractive wooded glen, by a burn on the left. On approaching the River Tweed, the path climbs a series of steps, turns right to continue high above the river and then descends along a stepped, zigzag path to a lane. Turn sharp left to cross a suspension footbridge over the river, and to the left appears the first of many grand views of the three Eildon peaks seen on this walk. On the other side follow a path to the right (**B**), which continues as a tarmac track and bears left uphill away from the river to a road in the small village of Dryburgh (**C**).

Keep ahead if visiting Dryburgh Abbey. The pink sandstone ruins are less complete than those of Jedburgh and Melrose but as compensation they lie in an incomparably beautiful and peaceful situation amidst lawns and old trees beside a bend in the Tweed. Like the other Border abbeys, it was founded by David I in the twelfth century and sacked by invading English armies in the middle of the sixteenth century. Within the remains of the church are the graves of two well-known Border names, Sir Walter Scott and Earl Haig.

The route continues to the left, heading uphill along the road. Where the road bends right, turn left, at a public footpath sign Wallace Monument, onto a tree-lined path that heads steadily uphill through woodland, finally turning sharp right to reach the red sandstone monument (**D**) to William Wallace, spirited Scottish patriot who led the resistance to Edward I's attempted conquest of Scotland before defeat in the Battle of Falkirk in 1298. Continue along the path that bends left past the monument through woodland and go through a gate to rejoin the road (**E**).

Turn left and follow this winding and steadily ascending road for 1 mile (1.5 km) up to Scott's View (**F**), 748 feet (229 m) up on the western slopes of Bemersyde Hill, the favourite viewpoint of Sir Walter Scott (1771–1832) who lived nearby. One can see why, for this is probably the finest view in southern Scotland, looking over a great horseshoe bend in the silvan Tweed with the three Eildon peaks perfectly framed in the background. A well-known story relates that Scott's horses were so used to stopping here that they did so out of habit while pulling his hearse to his burial place at Dryburgh Abbey.

Continue along the road, following it around a long left-hand bend. Where the road turns right, keep ahead (**G**) along a pleasant, straight, tree-lined lane, which later descends, bends to the right and continues down to a T-junction (**H**). Turn left along a road which curves left downhill, bends right to cross a bridge over Leader Water and continues to pass under a modern road bridge. Immediately turn left (**J**) over the oldest and lowest of the three bridges over the Tweed at Leaderfoot, dwarfed by its two neighbours to left and right. This bridge, the original road bridge but now a footbridge only, was built in the 1780s. The impressive nineteen-arched railway viaduct, now disused, was constructed in the 1860s and the modern road bridge in the 1970s.

Turn left along a road to the main A68 and turn right (**K**) along this busy road for

Scott's View – the Tweed valley and triple-peaked Eildon Hills

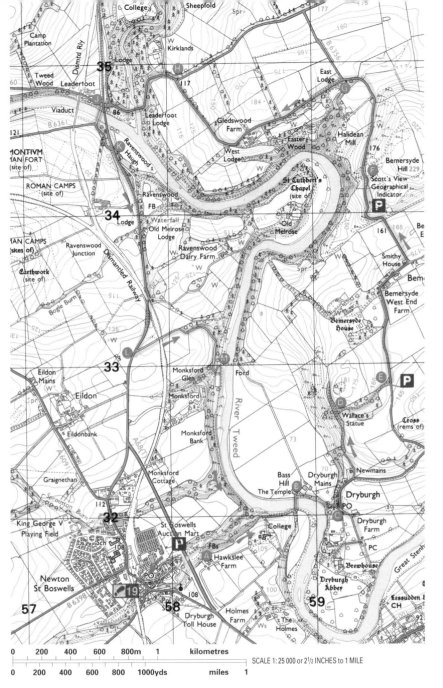

about ¾ mile (1.25 km) – there is a verge. Shortly after passing a layby on the right and a sign for Newtown St Boswells, turn sharp left (**L**) along a hedge-lined track that crosses a disused railway line and winds gently downhill. Continue along the right edge of conifer woodland and eventually curve sharply to the left to reach the river (**M**).

Turn right to follow a delightful path

beside the Tweed mainly below a steep wooded embankment on the right. A brief detour to the right is needed to cross a footbridge over Sprouston Burn, then the path turns left to rejoin the river and continues around a left curve to the next burn. Follow a path to the right through Bowden Glen and by the second footbridge you rejoin the outward route to retrace your steps to the start.

20 Broad Law

Start:	On road between Talla and Megget reservoirs just beyond Talla Bridge – turn off A701 at Tweedsmuir
Distance:	5½ miles (8.75 km)
Approximate time:	3 hours
Parking:	Roadside parking just beyond Talla Bridge
Refreshments:	None
Ordnance Survey maps:	Landranger 72 (Upper Clyde Valley), Pathfinder 471, NT 02/12 (Tweedsmuir)

General description At 2,755 feet (840 m) Broad Law is the highest peak in the Scottish Borders. This walk is a straightforward ascent and descent of it, keeping beside a fence all the way, and involves a steady and relatively easy climb as the starting point is over 1,400 feet (427 m) high. In fact, the final stretch is almost flat, and the rather featureless and undistinguished summit could be easily missed but for the triangulation pillar and Radio Beacon Station. All the way there are fine views over the smooth, empty, rolling expanses of the Tweedsmuir Hills. This walk is to be avoided in bad weather unless you are experienced in hillwalking in such conditions.

Start by walking eastward along the narrow road for ½ mile (0.75 km) as far as a cattle-grid. Turn left here (**A**) and keep beside a wire fence on the left all the way to the summit of Broad Law, a distance of 2¼ miles (3.75 km). For most of the way the path is clear and easy to follow.

The initial climb to Fans Law is the steepest part of the walk. Then comes a steady climb to Cairn Law, where the path bisects two cairns and follows the fence around left and right bends, and the final 1¼ miles (2 km) to Broad Law is gently uphill or at times flat walking along a smooth, broad, grassy ridge. The triangu-

The lonely valley of Talla Water from Broad Law

lation pillar and Radio Beacon Station just beyond are the only indications that you have arrived at the highest point in the Borders at 2,755 feet (840 m) (**B**). All the way there are fine views over bare and lonely hills with glimpses of Megget Reservoir and St Mary's Loch to the right.

Retrace your steps and on the descent you can enjoy the superb views in front of the valley of Talla Water. □

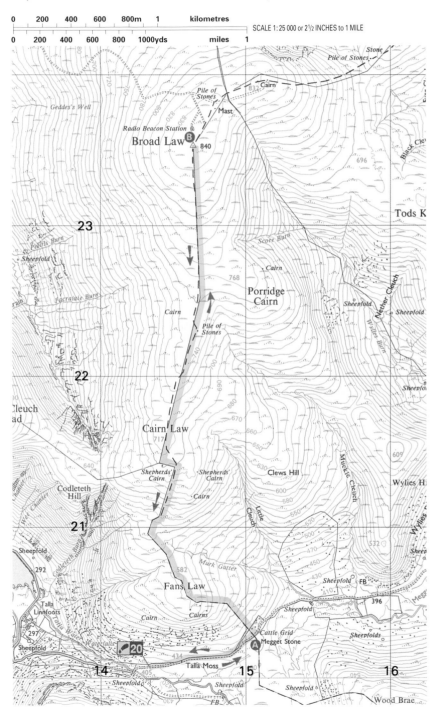

SCALE 1:25 000 or 2½ INCHES to 1 MILE

21 Caerketton and Allermuir hills

Start:	Hillend Ski Centre Country Park
Distance:	4½ miles (7.25 km)
Approximate time:	2½ hours
Parking:	Hillend Ski Centre
Refreshments:	Café at Ski Centre, pub at Hillend
Ordnance Survey maps:	Landranger 66 (Edinburgh & Midlothian), Pathfinder 420, NT 26/36 (Penicuik & Dalkeith)

General description The smooth, grassy slopes of the Pentland Hills to the south-west of Edinburgh provide excellent and quite demanding walking right on the edge of the city. This walk starts with a steep climb beside the Hillend artificial ski-slope to the summit of Caerketton Hill (1,502 feet)(458 m) and then continues along a switchback ridge to the higher Allermuir Hill (1,618 feet)(493 m). All the way there are magnificent and extensive views. After an easy descent, the return to Hillend takes you through the picturesque hamlet of Swanston.

From the car park take the steep uphill path, lined by wire fences to the right of the ski-slope and alongside a golf-course on the right. Climb a stile in the top corner of the golf-course, continue uphill across grass in the same direction as before – do not turn right alongside the golf-course fence or bear left to continue by a wire fence on the left – and, on meeting an obvious path, turn sharp left (**A**) and continue uphill, rejoining the wire fence bordering the ski-slope.

Follow the path up to the top of the ski-slope. Shortly afterwards it curves to the right away from the fence, heading more steeply uphill to meet a wire fence. Turn right alongside it up to a small cairn, descend and then climb again to reach the cairn on the summit of Caerketton Hill. The extensive views include Edinburgh, Arthur's Seat, Lothian coast, Bass Rock, Lammermuir Hills, the rest of the Pentlands and across the Firth of Forth to the hills of Fife.

Continue, alongside a wire fence on the left, along a winding and roller-coaster

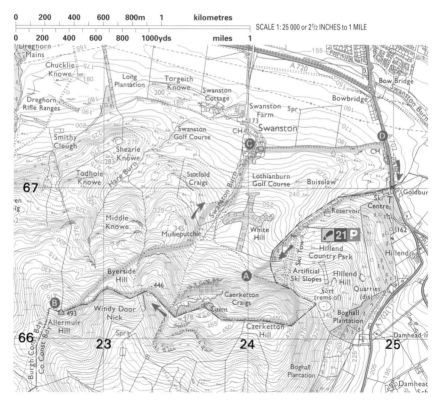

SCALE 1 : 25 000 or 2½ INCHES to 1 MILE

The thatched and whitewashed hamlet of Swanston nestles below the Pentland Hills

path across the smooth, grassy, heathery slopes, finally ascending steeply to the triangulation pillar and the National Trust for Scotland's view indicator on Allermuir Hill (**B**). This is another magnificent viewpoint.

Retrace your steps down into the first dip, where the path forks, and here leave the outward route to continue along the left-hand path that winds downhill between rough grass and heather, keeping below the sheer face of Caerketton Craigs on the right. At a junction of paths, just before reaching the corner of the golf-course, turn left at a waymarked post along a grassy path between gorse bushes. Arthur's Seat in Holyrood Park can be seen ahead in the distance. Take the right-hand, lower path at the next fork, continuing downhill between gorse and trees, and to the right is the aptly named T Wood, planted in the shape of a Greek cross in 1766 as a memorial to

a member of the Trotter family who died in battle.

The path bends right and heads down to a kissing-gate. Go through and follow it as it first bends to the right, then curves to the left to cross a footbridge over the tiny Swanston Burn, and curves left again, by a waymarked post, to continue down into Swanston. As a boy, Robert Louis Stevenson (1850–94) used to stay in this delightful hamlet of thatched and whitewashed cottages on the lower slopes of the Pentlands.

Go through a kissing-gate, keep ahead between cottages and turn right (**C**) along a tarmac drive. Go through another kissing-gate, continue along a track beside the left-hand edge of the golf-course, by a wire fence on the left, and go through a kissing-gate onto the main road (**D**). Turn right and, at the entrance to Hillend Ski Centre Country Park, turn right again to return to the start. ☐

22 Melrose and the Eildon Hills

Start:	Melrose
Distance:	5½ miles (8.75 km)
Approximate time:	3 hours
Parking:	Melrose
Refreshments:	Pubs and cafés at Melrose
Ordnance Survey maps:	Landranger 73 (Peebles & Galashiels), Pathfinder 461, NT 43/53 (Galashiels & Melrose)

General description *From almost all parts of the Border country, and indeed from a high proportion of the other walks in this book, the distinctive three peaks of the Eildon Hills can be seen, rising abruptly like a mini-mountain range above the Tweed valley. This walk climbs the two highest of these three peaks, both magnificent viewpoints, and after a steep descent into the village of Newstead finishes off with an attractive and relaxing stroll beside the River Tweed. Although not rising to any great height, the ascent of the Eildons is quite steep and tiring, but the paths are good, the route is well way-marked and the extensive views over Melrose, the Tweed valley and much of the Border country more than compensate for the effort. Leave plenty of time to visit Melrose Abbey, one of the finest monastic ruins in the country.*

The pleasant, small town of Melrose is dominated by the beautiful and extensive ruins of its abbey, built of the local pink sandstone and occupying a lovely setting on the south bank of the Tweed below the Eildons. The history of Melrose Abbey largely mirrors that of the other Border abbeys: founded by David I in 1136, repeatedly attacked and devastated by invading English armies and left in ruins after the last of these raids in the 1540s. It is, however, more complete and better

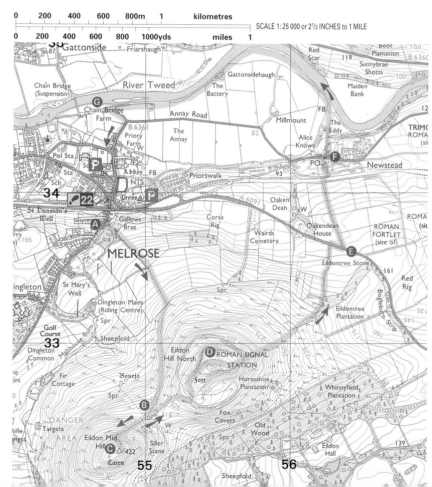

SCALE 1:25 000 or 2½ INCHES to 1 MILE

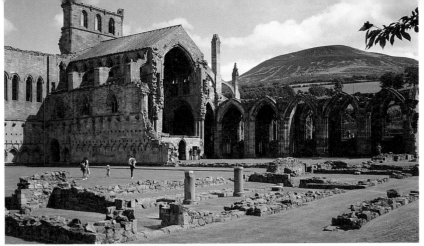

The ruins of Melrose Abbey occupy a lovely setting below the Eildons

preserved than most, especially the mainly fourteenth- and fifteenth-century church, the finest example in Scotland of the ornate Decorated style. The cloisters and domestic buildings are on the north side of the church, not as usual on the sunnier south side, probably because it was easier to use water from the Tweed for drainage and other purposes.

This is an easy route to follow as it is well-waymarked throughout with yellow arrows and 'Eildon Walk' signs. Start in Market Square and take the road sign-posted to Lilliesleaf, heading uphill and passing under the bypass bridge. About 100 yards (91 m) past the bridge, turn left, (A) at an Eildon Walk sign, go down steps and take the narrow uphill path ahead alongside the left-hand edge of wood-land. Bear right to ascend a long flight of steps and climb a stile at the top of them.

Head uphill, between wire fences, climb two stiles in quick succession and conti-nue up along the left-hand edge of a field, by a wire fence on the left, climbing an-other stile to emerge onto the open hill-side. Keep ahead to a footpath sign and turn right along a winding, steadily ascending path that reaches the gap between the North and Mid peaks of the Eildons. At a footpath sign, keep ahead for 50 yards (46 m) to a crossing of paths (B) and turn right for the steep ascent of Mid Hill (1,385 feet)(422 m). At the summit (C), a view indicator enables you to appreciate the tremendous panorama spread out before you. To the south is Wester Hill, the lowest of the three peaks at 1,216 feet (369 m).

Retrace your steps to the crossing of paths (B) and continue ahead to follow a clear, broad, winding track across heath-ery moorland up to the summit of North Hill (1,323 feet)(404 m) (D), a steady and less steep ascent. At the top are the re-mains of an Iron Age fort and a Roman signal station as well as another magni-ficent view, which includes Melrose down in the valley below, the winding Tweed, Mid and Wester hills and a large slice of the Border country.

At the summit cairn, bear left to con-tinue along the ridge and at a fork take the left-hand path – narrow but clear – that descends steeply between gorse and heather, making for a conifer plantation below. On reaching the conifers, keep along their left-hand edge down to a stile, climb it and continue down an enclosed, hedge- and tree-lined path to a road. Turn right, take the first track on the left (E) and follow it gently down, passing under a disused railway bridge, to a T-junction. Turn right along a track and turn left down Claymires Lane to the road in the village of Newstead (F).

Cross the road, continue along a tarmac track opposite – it later becomes a rough track – heading downhill, cross a footbridge over a narrow stream and shortly bear left to join the Tweed. Climb a stile and keep alongside the river, a most attractive stretch with fine views upstream. After the next stile you have to walk on top of a wall, known as the Battery Dyke – take care as it is quite narrow – and where the wall peters out, continue along a pleasant, partially tree- and hedge-lined path. To the left are attractive views of the Eildons and Melrose Abbey, and upstream a suspen-sion bridge can be seen.

After going through a metal gate, im-mediately turn left (G) along the left-hand edge of a field, by a fence and hedge on the left, and go through a kissing-gate on-to a lane. Turn left to a T-junction and turn right along a road, passing the entrance to the abbey and returning to Market Square.

23 Grey Mare's Tail and Loch Skeen

Start: National Trust for Scotland car park at Grey Mare's Tail

Distance: 6½ miles (10.5 km)

Approximate time: 4½ hours

Parking: Grey Mare's Tail

Refreshments: None

Ordnance Survey maps: Landranger 79 (Hawick & Eskdale), Pathfinder 483, NT 01/11 (White Coomb)

General description This is an energetic route with three steep climbs and some rough walking and boggy conditions in places. The steepest part comes right at the beginning along a well-constructed path beside the grand waterfall of the Grey Mare's Tail, before following the Tail Burn to the foot of the wild and lonely Loch Skeen. Then comes a circuit of the high ground around three sides of the loch, first climbing across rough, open moorland above its western shores to the magnificent viewpoint of Firthybrig Head, followed by a steep descent and then the third and final climb to Lochcraig Head. Finally, you descend along the eastern side to the foot of the loch again, here picking up your outward route. All the way there are extensive and impressive views over an austere landscape of rolling, empty hills. This walk should not be attempted in bad weather as route-finding could be difficult, especially in misty conditions.

Start by taking the stepped path on the right-hand side of the burn, signposted to Loch Skeen, that rises steeply above the Grey Mare's Tail to reach the top of the fall. This is the most strenuous part of the walk, however, from the path there are fine views of the waterfall. Continue along a rocky path above Tail Burn on the left through a wild and rugged landscape eventually to emerge suddenly at the foot of Loch Skeen (**A**), which appears abruptly in its austere setting, cradled by surrounding steep hills.

Grey Mare's Tail

Turn left to ford the burn at the outlet from the loch – there are plenty of large stones here. Then negotiate a boggy area on the far side and pick up a path through the heather that heads steeply up the hillside on the western side of the loch. Follow the path across the top, keeping away from the steep edge to the right, and continue in the same north-westerly direction, descending slightly and then climbing across open, rough, grassy moorland to reach a wall on Firthybrig Head (**B**). You should ideally aim to reach the wall where it bears right and another one joins it. From here there are magnificent and extensive views over the Border country, with Loch Skeen below.

Turn right alongside the wall, first heading down, then climbing steeply to Lochcraig Head, then descending steeply again. Keep beside the wall all the while, following it as it bends right and heads down towards the loch and taking care to avoid the wet, peaty sections. The wall later becomes a wire fence, and you keep beside it to where it turns left (**C**). At this point, head across the heather to the lochside and keep alongside it, picking up a discernible path, to reach the foot of the loch (**A**). Here you rejoin the outward route and retrace your steps to the starting point.

24 Kirk Yetholm and the Halterburn valley

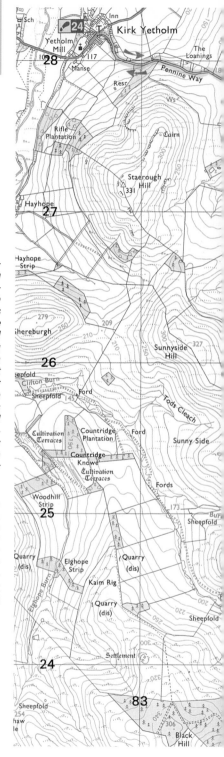

Start:	Kirk Yetholm
Distance:	8 miles (12.75 km)
Approximate time:	4½ hours
Parking:	Around the green at Kirk Yetholm
Refreshments:	Pub at Kirk Yetholm
Ordnance Survey maps:	Landranger 74 (Kelso), Pathfinder 475, NT 82/92 (The Cheviot Hills (North))

General description To walkers Kirk Yetholm is principally known as the northern terminus of the Pennine Way, the finishing point for the majority of people who walk it from south to north. This walk uses the last few miles of the Pennine Way, the outward route following the 'High-Level Main Route' and the return route using the 'Low-Level Alternative Route'. It is a reasonably energetic walk with quite a lot of climbing – lengthy and steady rather than steep and strenuous – over the smooth, grassy slopes of the Cheviots with extensive views across a rolling and largely empty landscape. Regular waymarking and clear paths make it an easy route to follow, especially as part of it is beside the fence that marks the border between Scotland and England.

Begin by taking the lane, signposted to Halterburn, that leads off from the green. The lane winds uphill and then descends to cross a cattle-grid by a Pennine Way finger-post (**A**). Turn left to ford Halter Burn by another finger-post – after heavy rain it will be advisable to use the footbridge about 100 yards (91 m) to the right – and head uphill by a wall on the left. Just before the wall ends, bear right to follow a path along the side of the valley across smooth, grassy slopes, keeping to the left of sheep pens and heading up to Stob Rig.

On reaching a wall, bear right (**B**) to continue alongside it. Apart from a few descents into hollows, the next 2 miles (3.25 km) are a virtually continuous uphill route that climbs several stiles and keeps beside the border fence – the double wire fence on the left that marks the Scottish-English border – all the time across Stob Rig, White Law and Steer Rig. It is a

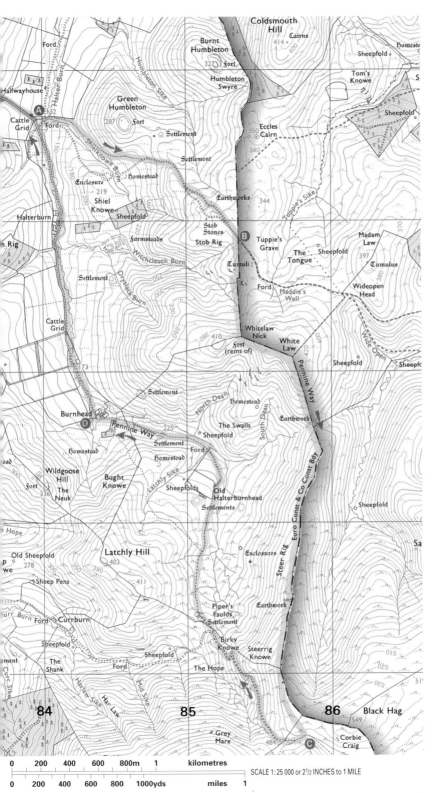

Coldsmouth
Hill
Cairns
414
400

Burnt
Humbleton
327 Fort
Humbleton
Swyre

Homeste

Sheepfold

Tom's
Knowe

Ford

Halfwayhouse

A 132

Green
Humbleton
287 Fort

Settlement

Settlement

Eccles
Cairn
350
340

Sheepfold

Cattle
Grid
Ford

Shielknowe Burn

160

Enclosure
219

Homestead

Shiel
Knowe

Sheepfold

Halterburn

Farmsteads

Witchcleuch Burn

Stob
Stones
Stob Rig

Earthworks
344

Tuppie's
Sike

B

Tuppie's
Grave
The
Tongue

Sheepfold

Madam
Law
397

Tumulus

Re Rig

Settlement

Dryden Burn

300

330

Tumuli

Ford
Maddie's
Well

Wideopen
Head

380

370

Cattle
Grid

173

410
380

Whitelaw
Nick
Fort
(rems of)

White
Law

400

Pennine Way

Wide Open

Sheepfold

Sheepfo

Burnhead

D

Settlement

Pennine Way
225

North Dean

Homestead

South Dean

Earthwork

The Swalls
Sheepfold

Settlement

Homestead

Ford

Old
Halterburnhead
Settlements

Euro Const & Co Const Bdy

Sheepfold

Homestead

Wildgoose
Hill
Fort
The
Neuk

Bught
Knowe

Latchly Sike

Sheepfolds

Hope

Old Sheepfold
278

Latchly Hill
403

Enclosures

Steer Rig

Sa

Sheep Pens

390

411

Earthwork

Sheepfold

urr Burn Ford

Currburn

Piper's
Faulds
Settlement

Earthwork

Sheepfold

The
Shank

Sheepfold

Birky
Knowe

Ford

Steerrig
Knowe

The Hope

520

51

510

530

84

85

86

Black Hag
1549

Curr Sike

Har Law

Harlaw Sike

Mid Sike

Grey
Mare
48

C

Corbie
Craig

0   200   400   600   800m   1   kilometres

0   200   400   600   800   1000yds   miles   1

SCALE 1:25 000 or 2½ INCHES to 1 MILE

63

The rolling, empty landscape of the Cheviots

magnificent ridge walk across an empty and open landscape, with fine views to the left over the Cheviots towards the Northumberland coast and to the right over the Scottish Border country with the three Eildon peaks prominent.

After you climb a ladder-stile, the border fence bears left, but you follow a path to the right to reach a junction of paths (**C**), where the High-Level Main Route and the Low-Level Alternative Route meet. Turn sharp right onto the low-level route, go through a kissing-gate and follow a winding path downhill. Go through another kissing-gate and continue to a ruined farm (Old Halterburnhead) near the first group of trees seen for a long while.

Here the Pennine Way turns left, becomes a track and continues through the valley above the burn. At a farm (Burnhead), keep to the left of the farm buildings and turn right (**D**) through a metal gate to continue along the track. The track soon becomes a tarmac lane, and you follow it past Halterburn to rejoin the outward route and retrace your steps to Kirk Yetholm. □

25 Traquair and Minch Moor

Start:	Traquair
Distance:	10 miles (16 km)
Approximate time:	5 hours
Parking:	By village hall at Traquair
Refreshments:	None
Ordnance Survey maps:	Landranger 73 (Peebles & Galashiels), Pathfinder 460, NT 23/33 (Innerleithen)

General description A steady climb along the ancient routeway of the Minchmoor Road, following part of the Southern Upland Way, leads to the summit of Minch Moor (1,860 feet)(567 m), a magnificent viewpoint over the Border country. This is followed by a descent through the conifers of Elibank and Traquair Forest and a walk through the pleasant valley of Bold Burn. The final leg is along a quiet lane below the forested slopes, partly beside the River Tweed. This is a superb combined hill, moorland and forest walk with splendid views but, despite clear and well-surfaced tracks throughout, not recommended in misty conditions.

Refer to map overleaf.

The walk starts at the war memorial, where you follow the direction of a Southern Upland Way sign along a lane, passing the village hall on the left. Head uphill and, where the lane bends right, continue along the track ahead, signposted Minchmoor.

Follow the track, initially enclosed between walls, steadily uphill, climbing several stiles and going through a number of gates. There are grand views over the Tweed valley. Later the track enters the conifers of Elibank and Traquair Forest and eventually emerges onto the open heathery expanses of Minch Moor. Look out for the Cheese Well by a small stream.

The summit of Minch Moor

Ascending Minch Moor above the Tweed valley

A notice states that cattle-drovers used to drop pieces of cheese into the well to gain the favour of the fairies haunting this spot and thus guarantee a safe journey. Continue across the moor and, just before the next group of conifers, a track leads off to the right (**A**) gently uphill to the triangulation pillar and cairn on the summit of Minch Moor (**B**). This brief detour is well worth while for the magnificent all-round view of the encircling hills.

Retrace your steps and turn right to continue along the Southern Upland Way. Descend gently to a crossing of tracks and here turn left (**C**) off the Minchmoor Road and Southern Upland Way to continue along a broad track that curves left through the forest, heading gently downhill. The track later bends right across the slopes of Bold Rig. On meeting another track, turn sharp right along it (**D**) to head gently downhill to a junction of tracks.

Here turn sharp left, (**E**) almost doubling back, along a track through the valley of Bold Burn, a pleasant route mainly along the left-hand edge of conifers, with fine views of the Tweed valley. At a fork, continue along the left-hand track, go through a gate and pass between Forestry Commission chalets to reach a lane (**F**).

Turn left and follow the lane for nearly 3 miles (4.75 km) back to the start, an attractive and relaxing finale, passing below some delightful sloping woodland on the left and later keeping above the Tweed on the right. Finally join the B709 for the last ¾ mile (1.25 km) to Traquair. □

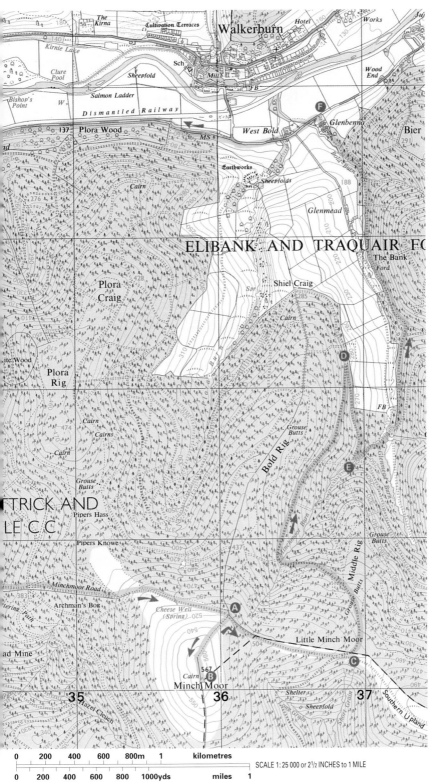

The Kirna

Cultivation Terraces

Walkerburn

Hotel

Works

Kirnie Lake

Clure Pool

Sch

Mill

FB

Wood End

Bishop's Point

Sheepfold

Salmon Ladder

W

Dismantled Railway

MS

West Bold

Glenbenna

Bier

137 Plora Wood

Earthworks

Sheepfolds

188

Glenmead

ELIBANK AND TRAQUAIR FO

The Bank

Ford

Cairn

Plora Craig

428

Shiel Craig

Spr

285

Cairn

ite Wood

474

Plora Rig

D

FB

Cairn

474

Cairns

Grouse Butts

Bold Rig

Cairn

Grouse Butts

E

**TRICK AND
LE C.C**

Pipers Hass

Grouse Butts

Pipers Knowe

437

Middle Rig

Grouse Butts

Minchmoor Road

383

Archman's Bog

Cheese Well
(Spring)

A

Little Minch Moor

ad Mine

C

Cairn

567

B

Southern Upland

Minch Moor

Shelter

Sheepfold

35

36

37

0   200   400   600   800m   1   kilometres

SCALE 1: 25 000 or 2½ INCHES to 1 MILE

0   200   400   600   800   1000yds   miles   1

26 Minchmoor Road and the Three Brethren

Start:	Yarrowford
Distance:	8 miles (12.75 km)
Approximate time:	4½ hours
Parking:	Parking area beside road at Yarrowford
Refreshments:	None
Ordnance Survey maps:	Landranger 73 (Peebles & Galashiels), Pathfinders 460, NT 23/33 (Innerleithen), 461, NT 43/53 (Galashiels & Melrose) and 473, NT 42/52 (Selkirk)

General description *Using two old drove roads, this exhilarating hill and moorland walk starts by the River Yarrow and ascends the Minchmoor Road to the ridge between the Yarrow and Tweed valleys. Then comes a grand undulating walk along the ridge, with magnificent views all around, following part of the Southern Upland Way to reach the prominent landmark of the Three Brethren. Finally, the route descends, with more fine views, back into the Yarrow valley. This is quite a strenuous walk with plenty of long and steady climbs but route-finding is generally easy on clear, well-surfaced and well-waymarked tracks, except for the immediate descent from the Three Brethren, where the directions have to be read carefully. However, this walk is not recommended in misty weather.*

Refer to map overleaf.

With your back to the river, turn left along the road and after a few yards take the tarmac lane to the right, at a public footpath sign Innerleithen via Minchmoor. After passing the last of the houses, the lane becomes a rough track, which bends left uphill, then bends sharp right and, on the edge of woodland, turns left again (**A**) to continue uphill between an avenue of impressive old trees.

Now follows a steady, unremitting, lengthy but not strenuous climb along the Minchmoor Road – a winding, clear and well-drained track from which there are splendid open views across empty, rolling countryside. After 2¼ miles (3.75 km) you reach a T-junction of tracks (**B**) on

the edge of conifer forest by a Southern Upland Way marker-post bearing a white thistle.

Turn sharp right to follow the Southern Upland Way for 3½ miles (5.5 km) along a superb ridge path – an undulating route that crosses heather and grass moorland over Brown Knowe and Broomy Law with more magnificent views across to the Yarrow valley on the right and the Tweed valley on the left. You finally head uphill to the right of a conifer plantation to reach the distinctive tall cairns of the Three

Brethren (**C**) seen on the skyline in front. From here there are extensive views over the hills, valleys and forests of the Border country with the three peaks of the Eildons especially prominent. The Three Brethren – three tall, identical cairns, built to mark the boundary of three estates – crown a 1,523-foot- (464 m) high hill.

At the Three Brethren, turn right – not on the Southern Upland Way, which continues to the left of a wire fence – but on a narrow but discernible path to the right of that fence, which heads downhill through heather, veering right away from the fence. After descending into a small hollow, look out for a heathery path, seen curving away to the right – this is not easy to spot – turn right (**D**) along it and you soon reach a gate in a wire fence. Go through the gate and continue along a much more obvious path that descends gently to ford a small burn and then curves left to head steadily over the shoulder of Foulshiels Hill. Over the brow of the hill, a superb view unfolds over the Yarrow valley with the hamlet of Yarrow-

Rolling hills cradle the Yarrow valley near Yarrowford

ford below. Descend on what by now has become a track, winding downhill to reach the edge of a conifer plantation (**E**).

Turn left downhill along a track parallel to a wall bordering the conifers on the right, passing through three gates to reach a road. On this descent there is a view of Newark Castle ahead, originally

built in the fifteenth century by James II as a royal hunting-lodge in Ettrick Forest. Turn sharp right (**F**) along the road to return to the start, crossing the Yarrow twice and following the river for the last ¼ mile (0.5 km). Take care here as there is no footpath and there are only narrow verges. ☐

27 Pentland Ridge

Start:	Threipmuir Reservoir. From Balerno follow signs to Marchbank, and car park is on the left, near where the road ends
Distance:	7½ miles (12 km)
Approximate time:	4½ hours
Parking:	Threipmuir
Refreshments:	None
Ordnance Survey maps:	Landranger 66 (Edinburgh & Midlothian), Pathfinder 419, NT 06/16 (Livingston & Currie)

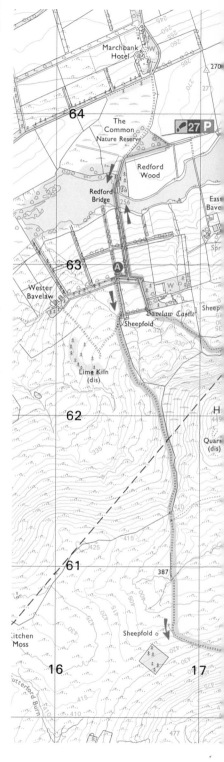

General description *A long but gradual climb from Threipmuir Reservoir across open grassland leads to the main, central ridge of the Pentland Hills and then follows a splendid but quite strenuous switchback walk over three peaks: West Kip, East Kip and finally Scald Law (1,898 feet) (579 m), the highest point in the Pentland range. As might be expected, the views from the ridge path – to the left across the Pentlands to the Firth of Forth and to the right across the lowlands to the Lammermuir Hills – are magnificent. The descent from Scald Law is followed by an attractive walk through the narrow and steep-sided valley of Green Cleugh to return to the start. This is a most enjoyable and exhilarating walk with plenty of steep climbing and superb views but definitely one to be avoided in bad weather, especially mist, unless you are experienced in such conditions and able to navigate by using a compass.*

Turn left out of the car park along a track and, after a few yards where the track bears left, turn sharp right along a path through trees. On reaching a tarmac drive opposite a notice for Red Moss Nature Reserve, turn left along it to cross Redford Bridge over Threipmuir Reservoir.

Continue along the lovely, uphill beech drive ahead and at a T-junction of tracks (**A**) turn right, at a public footpath sign Nine Mile Burn and Carlops. After going through a gate, turn left along a drive to a stile, climb it and continue along a track, by a wall and wire fence bordering woodland on the left, to climb another one. Now follow a track gently uphill, keeping

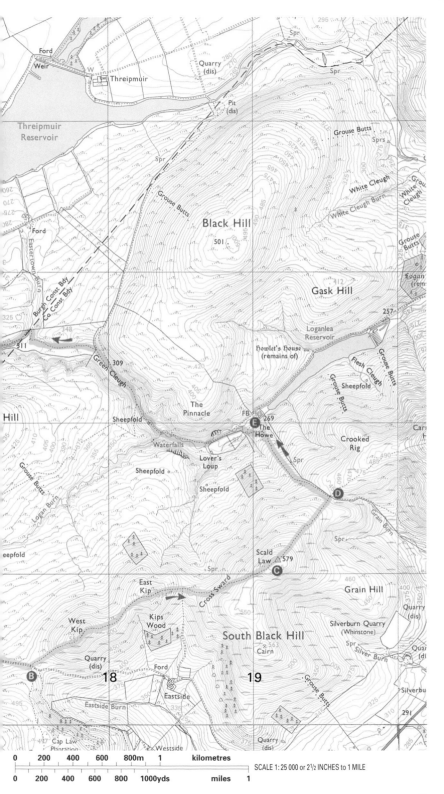

Ford
Weir
Threipmuir
Threipmuir
Reservoir
Quarry (dis)
Pit (dis)
Grouse Butts
Sprs
White Cleugh
White Cleugh Burn
White Cleugh
Grou
Cleugh
Ford
Black Hill
501
Grouse Butts
Grouse Butts
Easterton Burn
Burgh Const Bdy
Co Const Bdy
Gask Hill
412
Loganlea Reservoir
257
Logan
(rem
348
325
511
309
Green Cleugh
420
Howlet's House (remains of)
Flesh Cleugh
Grouse Butts
Sheepfold
Grouse Butts
Hill
Sheepfold
The Pinnacle
FB
269
E The Howe
Carr
Crooked Rig
490
485
485
Waterfalls
Lover's Loup
Sheepfold
Spr
D
Grain Burn
Sheepfold
Grouse Butts
Logan Burn
475
C Scald Law △ 579
Spr
460
Grain Hill
400
East Kip
Cross Sward
550
Quarry (dis)
West Kip
Kips Wood
563
South Black Hill
Cairn
Silverburn Quarry (Whinstone)
Spr
Silver Burn
Quar (di
Quarry (dis)
B
18
Ford
Eastside
19
Grouse Butts
Silverbu
291
496
Eastside Burn
Quarry (dis)
325
310
285
Cap Law Plantation
Westside
375

0   200   400   600   800m   1   kilometres
0   200   400   600   800   1000yds   miles   1

SCALE 1:25 000 or 2½ INCHES to 1 MILE

Approaching the main ridge of the Pentland Hills

parallel to a wall on the left, onto the open, rolling, heathery expanses of the Pentlands, with grand views of the main Pentland ridge. The track leads up to a gate and footpath sign. Go through, continue to cross a burn and shortly head up more steeply, bending left towards the first of the summits, West Kip.

On reaching a stile in a wire fence on the right, bear left onto a path (**B**) that heads steeply and dauntingly up the smooth, grassy slopes of West Kip. At the top is the reward of a magnificent view that takes in the Pentland ridge, Firth of Forth, Lothian lowlands and Lammermuir and Moorfoot hills. From here the path descends and then ascends – rather less steeply – to the summit of East Kip. Then follows a steep descent to a fork. Here take the left-hand path to climb steeply again to the triangulation pillar on the summit of Scald Law (**C**), the highest point in the Pentlands and an even more magnificent viewpoint.

Continue past the triangulation pillar and head steeply down into the next dip below the slopes of Carnethy Hill. Where paths cross (**D**), climb a stile and turn left to head steeply downhill, by a wire fence

on the left, to a ladder-stile. Climb it, continue along the path that curves right to another stile, climb that and keep ahead steeply downhill. Nearing the bottom, the path swings left down to a stile. Climb it, by a public footpath sign Old Kirk Road to Penicuik, keep ahead and turn left at a fence corner (**E**) along a path by a burn on the right. There is a path on each side of the burn – take your pick as either will involve at least one fording.

Continue through the narrow, peaceful, steep-sided valley of Green Cleugh, climbing gently to reach a ladder-stile. Turn left over it to continue along the right-hand side of the valley – the sides are less steep now – climb another ladder-stile and continue towards the trees ahead. The path turns left to cross two planks over marshy ground and winds past two waymarked posts to a ladder-stile on the edge of the trees, by a public footpath sign Penicuik, Colinton and Flotterstone.

Climb the stile and continue along a beech drive, following it first to the left and shortly around to the right. Here you rejoin the outward route to retrace your steps to the start. ☐

28 Clints Dod, Herring Road and Dunbar Common

Start:	Woodland Trust's Pressmennan Wood car park. From Stenton, take the lane signposted to Deuchrie and, just after Rucklaw West Mains Farm, turn left onto a track at a 'Forest Trail Car Park' sign
Distance:	11 miles (17.5 km)
Approximate time:	5½ hours
Parking:	Pressmennan Wood
Refreshments:	None
Ordnance Survey maps:	Landranger 67 (Duns, Dunbar & Eyemouth), Pathfinders 409, NT 67/77 (Dunbar) and 422, NT 66/76 (Abbey St Bathans)

General description *The Lammermuir Hills are a range of rolling, open, heathery moorlands, rising to over 1,700 feet (518 m) and from their northern slopes there are superb and extensive views over the fertile lowlands of Lothian and along the North Sea coast. This walk over the Lammermuirs is a lengthy but not strenuous walk as all the ascents and descents are long and gradual, and most of the route is along clear and well-surfaced tracks, with just two difficult sections where the track degenerates into a rough, faint and uneven path. It is exhilarating to walk across these wide and empty expanses, and the views are magnificent, but this is a walk best reserved for a fine and clear day; in bad weather and misty conditions route-finding could be difficult in places.*

Refer to map overleaf.

Start by walking back along the track to the lane, turn left and follow it for 1 mile (1.5 km) around several sharp bends and over a ford. At a row of cottages on the left, turn left (**A**) along an uphill tarmac drive to Stoneypath Farm and by the farm turn right through a metal gate, at a public footpath sign to Johnscleugh, to continue along a steadily ascending track. Ahead are grand views over the smooth, heathery slopes of the Lammermuirs, a fore-taste of pleasures to come.

Follow the track steadily uphill over Clints Dod. Cross a track just to the right of a house, continue by a wire fence on the left, go through a gate and proceed over the open moorland. After reaching the summit – virtually imperceptible – the track descends gently to a gate. Go through and continue steadily downhill into the Whiteadder valley. Go through a gate, keep ahead to pass between the buildings of Johnscleugh Farm and continue along a downhill track. Where the track bends sharply to the right, keep ahead steeply downhill, cross a plank over a ditch and go through the gate ahead. Ford Whiteadder Water – might be difficult after a rainy spell – and continue along an uphill path to a lane (**B**).

Turn left for ½ mile (0.75 km) above the winding Whiteadder Water and, just after first a left- and then a right-hand bend, you reach a ford beyond which is a cattle-grid (**C**). Here turn left along a broad track; this is the Herring Road, an ancient route-way across the hills that linked the fishing port of Dunbar with its markets inland.

The wide, empty, heathery expanses of the Lammermuirs

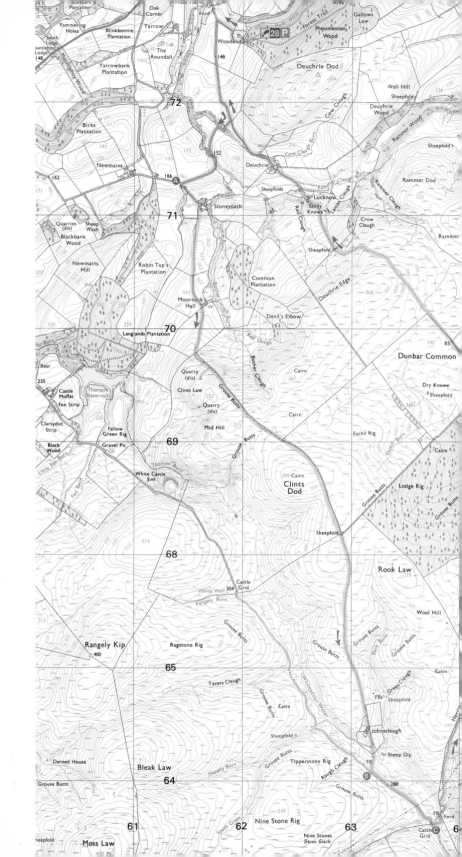

Recross the Whiteadder, this time by a footbridge, go through a gate and continue along the broad, winding, uphill track. The track later straightens out and, where it bends right, continue by a wire fence on the left across the moorland. Go through a gate, keep ahead and, after the fence turns left, continue across rough grass to join and walk along a clear, well-constructed track again.

A few yards after going through a gate to the right of a small group of conifers, the track bears right. Keep straight ahead here across rough grass and heather to climb a stile by a public footpath sign. Continue in the same direction, following a broad swathe of heather and rough grass through a young conifer plantation to reach a stony track by two public footpath signs. Cross the track, continue along a reasonably discernible path through the young conifers and, soon after descending to cross a small burn, head up a steep embankment to a public footpath sign in front of a metal gate and by a fence corner and broken wall. Go through the gate and continue uphill, by a wire fence on the left, to the fence corner.

Turn left (**D**), here leaving the Herring Road, to walk across open moorland along a grassy path by a fence, still bordering a plantation on the left. At the corner of the plantation, go through a gate and keep ahead, still by a wire fence on the left, across the wide-open expanses of Dunbar Common. Go through a metal gate, continue and, after the fence on the left ends, keep straight ahead across moorland. At this point the path is unclear in places, and there is some rough and difficult walking, but keep in a straight line all the while until a discernible path reappears, and later still a clear, grassy track emerges. All the way there are magnificent views across the lowlands to the coast, with both North Berwick Law and Traprain Law standing out prominently.

Eventually the grassy track heads downhill, curving left and descending more steeply to go through a fence gap to the right of a circular sheepfold. Continue downhill, pass to the left of a house to reach a gate, go through and head uphill to Deuchrie Farm. Go through a metal gate, pass between the house and farm buildings and continue along a tarmac drive to reach a lane at a bend. Retrace your steps to the start. □

0   200   400   600   800m   1   Kilometres

0   200   400   600 yds   ½ mile

SCALE 1:33 333 or about 2 INCHES to 1 MILE

Useful organisations

Association for the Protection of Rural Scotland
Gladstone's Land, 483 Lawnmarket,
Edinburgh EH1 2NT. Tel: 0131 225 7012

Borders Regional Council
Newtown St Boswells, Melrose TD6 0SA.
Tel: 01835 23301

Forestry Commission
Information Branch, 231 Corstorphine Road,
Edinburgh EH12 7AT. Tel: 0131 334 0303

Historic Scotland
Long House, Salibury Place,
Edinburgh EH9 1SH. Tel: 0131 244 3101

Long Distance Walkers' Association
7 Ford Drive, Yarnfield,
Stone, Staffordshire ST15 0RP

Lothian Regional Council
12 St Giles' Street, Edinburgh EH1 1PT.
Tel: 0131 229 9292

National Trust for Scotland
5 Charlotte Square, Edinburgh EH2 4DU.
Tel: 0131 226 5922

Ordnance Survey
Romsey Road, Southampton SO16 4GU.
Tel: 01703 792912

Ramblers' Association (Scotland)
23 Crusader House, Haig Business Park,
Markinch, Fife KY7 6AQ. Tel: 01592 611177

Scottish Borders Tourist Board
70 High Street, Selkirk TD7 4DD.
Tel: 01750 20555

Scottish Natural Heritage
Information and Library Services,
2/5 Anderson Place,
Edinburgh EH6 5NP.
Tel: 0131 554 9797

Scottish Rights of Way Society Ltd
John Cotton Business Centre,
10/2 Sunnyside, Edinburgh EH7 5RA.
Tel: 0131 652 2937

Scottish Wildlife Trust
25 Johnston Terrace,
Edinburgh EH1 2NH.
Tel: 0131 226 4602

Scottish Youth Hostels Association
7 Glebe Terrace,
Stirling FK8 2JA.
Tel: 01786 51181

Tourist information centres in this area:
Bonnyrigg. Tel: 0131 660 6814
Dalkeith. Tel: 0131 660 6818
Dunbar. Tel: 01368 63353
Edinburgh. Tel: 0131 557 1700
Jedburgh. Tel: 01835 863435
Linlithgow. Tel: 01506 844600
North Berwick. Tel: 01620 2197
Old Craighill. Tel: 0131 653 6172
Penicuik. Tel: 01968 72340

Weather forecasts:
For Scotland, 48-hour forecast. Tel: 0891 112260
UK seven-day forecast. Tel: 0891 333123

Ordnance Survey maps of Edinburgh and the Borders

Edinburgh and the Borders are covered by Ordnance Survey 1:50 000 scale (1¼ inches to 1 mile or 2 cm to 1 km) Landranger map sheets 57, 58, 65, 66, 67, 71, 72, 73, 74, 78, 79, 80, 85 and 86.

These all-purpose maps are packed with information to help you explore the areas. Viewpoints, picnic sites, places of interest and caravan and camping sites are shown as well as information such as footpaths and bridleways (rights-of-way in England and Wales only).

To examine this area in more detail, and especially if you are planning walks, the Ordnance Survey Pathfinder maps at 1:25 000 scale (2½ inches to 1 mile or 4 cm to 1 km) are ideal, maps covering this area are:

383 (NS 89/99)	395 (NT 28)
451 (NT 84/94)	460 (NT 23/33)
393 (NS 88/98)	396 (NT 48/58/68)
458 (NS 83/93)	461 (NT 43/53)
394 (NT 08/18)	405 (NT 87/97)
459 (NT 03/13)	462 (NT 63/73)

406 (NT 07/17)	433 (NT 05/15)
463 (NT 83/93)	486 (NT 61/71)
408 (NT 47/57)	434 (NT 25/35)
470 (NS 82/92)	494 (NS 80/90)
407 (NT 27/37)	435 (NT 45/55)
471 (NT 02/12)	495 (NT 00/10)
409 (NT 67/77)	436 (NT 65/75)
472 (NT 22/32)	496 (NT 20/30)
418 (NS 86/96)	437 (NT 85)
473 (NT 42/52)	497 (NT 40/50)
419 (NT 06/16)	438 (NT 95/NU05)
474 (NT 62/72)	498 (NT 60/70)
420 (NT 26/36)	446 (NS 84/94)
475 (NT 82/92)	507 (NY 29/39)
421 (NT 46/56)	447 (NT 04/14)
482 (NS 81/91)	508 (NY 49/59)
422 (NT 66/76)	448 (NT 24/34)
483 (NT 01/11)	519 (NY 28/38)
423 (NT 86/96)	449 (NT 44/54)
484 (NT 21/31)	520 (NY 48/58)
432 (NS 85/95)	450 (NT 64/74)
485 (NT 41/51)	532 (NY 47/57)

To get to this region use the Ordnance Survey Great Britain Routeplanner (Travelmaster map number 1) or Travelmaster map number 4, Central Scotland and Northumberland.

Ordnance Survey maps and guides are available from most booksellers, stationers and newsagents.

Index